Fetched-up Yankee

FETCHED-UP YANKEE

A New England Boyhood Remembered

by
Lewis Hill

The Globe Pequot Press

Chester, Connecticut

Library of Congress
Hill, Lewis, 1924–
    Fetched-up Yankee : a New England boyhood remembered / by Lewis
Hill.—1st ed.
        p.   cm.
    ISBN 0-87106-425-1
    1. Vermont—Social life and customs. 2. Vermont—Rural conditions. 3.
Hill, Lewis, 1924– —Childhood and youth. 4. Vermont—Biography.
I. Title.
F54.H55   1990
974.3'042'092—dc20
[B]   90-34998
                                                          CIP

Manufactured in the United States of America
First Edition/First Printing

To the memory of Calvin Coolidge,
the perfect example of a well-fetched-up Yankee.

CONTENTS

PREFACE

If ever there was a true Yankee woman, surely Effie Cheever qualified. In true New England fashion, she never hunted around for the best words to express her feelings; instead, she shot out her thoughts in plain language no one could possibly misunderstand. One day while my family was visiting her, my mother reminded me to take off my cap in the house. "Conscience yes, boy," exclaimed the plump old Mrs. Cheever. "Hain't you had no fetching up?"

Since I was only four at the time, I would probably have completely forgotten the incident, especially since Effie soon passed around a plate of freshly made doughnuts; but my brothers and sisters never let me. Years later, whenever I misbehaved, I was always reprimanded with Effie's phrase.

Proper "fetching up" was very important in our area during the 1930s when the way that children were raised was carefully observed by the entire neighborhood, and parents who appeared to be failing at their job were severely criticized. People lived according to decades of strait-laced tradition, and few dared to defy it. Embroidered proverbs extolling work and honesty hung in frames on everyone's kitchen wall. In case we didn't absorb them there, we were made to memorize them in school: "All that you do, do with your might, things done by halves are never done right"; "early to bed, early to rise, makes a man healthy, wealthy and wise"; "never leave 'til tomorrow that which you can do today." Long before we could comprehend the meaning of the verses, we could all recite them in sing-song voices.

Indoctrination from the cradle on made us realize that no one should expect to spend his threescore years and ten being happy, nor was it wise to waste time by making others happy. Work and worry were the way of life, and encouragement and compliments were seldom given. People were expected to do their work well and behave themselves, and certainly no congratulations were in order for doing that.

Hard work was not only necessary, but it was also noble; and to avoid it would lead to disgrace, dishonor, and probably, eventually, to Hell itself. If a true Yankee ran out of work, he was expected to look for more. What constituted real work was clearly defined, and in numerous ways it was pointed out that those who taught, sold merchandise, lent money, or otherwise worked with their brains and mouths were to be held in far less esteem than those who did hard physical labor. A suspicion of outsiders and of the outside world was firmly implanted in us, and we were told frequently that a body was "better off staying t' home where he b'longed, and shouldn't ought to go gallivanting all over Creation."

We were taught to expect the worst and to be surprised when things turned out all right. If someone was sick, a neighbor could always recollect a relative who had drawn his last breath from a similar ailment. No one ever mentioned the brilliant fall colors of the maples without pointing out that a hard winter was on the way.

A genuine New Englander learned by example never to take anything for granted. Once, when I remarked that it was a nice day, my Uncle Henry looked up at the sky, turned in every direction, and seeing that there wasn't a cloud anywhere, took the pipe from his mouth and finally conceded, "Well, maybe."

Driving up to the gas pumps at the general store, my older brother always got out, took off the gas cap, and waited for someone to come out. Inevitably when the elderly storekeeper finally appeared, he first looked sternly at the car and next at the cap in my brother's hand. Then, with his pipe still clenched tightly in his teeth, he would ask accusingly in a loud voice, "You want gas?"

If you asked someone if he had a watch, he would probably answer "Yes," but he wouldn't tell you the time unless you made a specific request. Likewise, an "Outlander" would not get much help from such questions as "Can you tell me the way to Montpelier?" or "Does John Bush live near here?" "A-ya" or "Nope" were likely to be the cryptic responses.

We were taught to settle our problems without recourse to police, lawyers, or courts. When Rob Carrie promised George Tyler he would pay him everything he owed by Thursday if he lived, George knew from experience that repayment was highly unlikely. Thursday came and went, "just as he knowed it would," and Friday afternoon, George appeared on the Carrie threshold all gusseyed up in his Sunday suit, clean shaven and with his hair neatly parted in the middle.

"Why, Mr. Tyler," cried the excited Mrs. Carrie in her rich Scottish burr. "Where in the world be ye goin' all dressed up like a banty rooster?"

"Why, I came to Rob's funeral," said George sadly.

"What do you mean, funeral?" Mrs. Carrie demanded. "Rob hain't dead. He's right down there in the field mowing oats."

"He ain't dead?" Now George looked astonished. "Why, he said he'd pay yesterday if'n he lived, and he didn't so I figgered he musta died."

Rob went over to the Tylers' with a check that evening. Mrs. Carrie saw to that.

Euphemism abounded. In proper Victorian language that deplored crudeness, we learned that a bull was either a "gentleman cow" or a "critter." People didn't die; they "passed away" or "went to their glory." Manure was fertilizer, arms and legs were limbs, and a pregnant woman was described as being "that way," "in you-know-what condition," or "unlikely to be seen out in public for a few months." Sex was only hinted at, even though cattle, chickens, dogs, and cats kept it constantly displayed on every farm.

Keeping one's pride was extremely important. Because borrowing money sounded like begging, a farmer could never walk into a bank and ask for a loan. Instead he'd "be much obliged to hire some money for a few months, or sech a matter." Likewise, Fred Cheever never broke any of the tools he borrowed from us. They always "broke" when they were with him.

Not only our family and schoolteachers made sure we got proper fetching up, but the neighbors felt it was their duty to lecture us frequently. Furthermore, they dutifully kept our parents and everyone else informed of any transgressions seen or imagined.

But times were beginning to change, and the twentieth century was arriving—though thirty years late. The newfangled radio, the corrupting automobile, and the telephone were making "proper fetching up" an increasingly difficult job. Hordes of New Yorkers vacationing in our town brought some shameful customs with them. One local lady who lived near the village complained that she no longer looked forward to summer, "what with those wretched city women driving cars, wearing war paint, smoking cigarettes and lolligagging about the village in shorts, showing off their bare limbs."

Although the changes were shocking and painful to the stubborn old Yankees, it was an exciting time to be young. As the boy said when he got his first kiss in a covered bridge, I wouldn't have missed it for anything.

FETCHED-UP YANKEE

THE FRONT SEAT

"You are a very lucky little boy," my mother and my older brothers and sisters told me many times the week before I began my formal education, "to have such a nice new school to go to."

Actually the one-room schoolhouse was 100 years old, but they meant that two or three years earlier—just before the Depression—some major changes had been made. The two smelly old outhouses had been replaced by indoor chemical toilets. Two separate entrances, one for boys and one for girls, had been removed and a new central front door installed. Most wonderful of all, the old pot-bellied stove that had baked the front half of the room when it was red hot had been supplanted by a modern, wood-burning jacketed heater.

Like most rural schoolhouses, it had no running water, and the nearest electricity was several miles and about ten years away. Since the schoolhouse renovations had been completed, hard times had moved off Wall Street and into our town and settled down, as if for a long stay. Any further luxuries, including new books, were unlikely.

Ma briefed me thoroughly on proper behavior before I started out alone that September morning on my first long mile to school. She probably had misgivings and maybe a few regrets about sending her youngest out into the world, but I was too excited and apprehensive to notice. The rest of my family added so many dos and don'ts to her warnings that I couldn't possibly remember them all. School was obviously filled with pitfalls.

Before I had walked a scant quarter mile from home, my troubles began. Right in the middle of the road, Sam and Mary Twists' big red rooster blocked my way. I had been warned repeatedly about wild animals and bulls, but no one ever had mentioned poultry. Chickens were no novelty to me, because we had a flock on our dairy farm, but our White Leghorns were a small, nervous breed that seemed afraid of their own shadows. The huge, brightly colored Rhode Island Red in front of me was drawn up to his full height, which seemed approximately eight feet. He strutted around the middle of the dirt road as if he had just bought the world beyond, and he cockily dared me to proceed.

Since I had to either walk past him or crawl over several fences and wade through a swamp, I had little choice. I edged by him slowly, and holding my lunch pail tightly, started to run. He, naturally, gave chase, caught up swiftly, and began to peck furiously at my arms and jab at my bare legs with his sharp spurs. Racing at top speed, I finally got out of his territory, thus causing him to stop the assault and return to his hen harem. Glancing back, I could see him fly to the top of a fence post, where he started crowing his brags at the top of his lungs, while I used my brand-new handkerchief to wipe the blood from my legs and arms.

Things didn't look so good now, and my confidence at meeting the outside world was badly shaken. In addition to the unknown adventures ahead at school, I now had the prospect of facing that old feathered fiend twice each day. I walked more slowly, still tightly gripping the metal lunch pail; and knowing it was well filled with food I liked, I began to feel more secure. There were two sandwiches made with thick slices of homemade bread—one spread with rhubarb conserve, and another with wild raspberry jam. The box also held a boiled egg, a raisin-filled cookie, a piece of frosted cake, and a small thermos of milk. At least I could look forward to lunch.

Everyone arrived early the first day, and eighteen children seemed to fill the small schoolyard to overflowing. I was overwhelmed by the large crowd, most of whom I'd never seen before. The boys were dressed in shorts, as I was, or in knickers or overalls, and a couple of them were barefoot. The girls wore clean, starched dresses, and one wore an apron. Most of us had recently received a home haircut, some obviously by the bowl-over-the-head method.

Because many of the children looked alike, it was clear that they were closely related, and I learned later that five of them were from the same family. That was no surprise, as large families were the rule in our neighborhood. I was the youngest of eleven children, and my father had died a few months after I was born. Only recently had I begun to realize that I surprised my parents, arriving after my brothers and sisters had pretty much grown up.

Although the schoolyard was full, it was quiet. The children stared at one another, and the boys especially were sizing one another up, trying to determine who had grown big enough over the summer to merit respect and who could still be shoved around. I was quickly spotted as the only new kid and was aware that a lot of eyes were looking me over closely. I was grateful when one tall girl told me to put my lunch pail just inside the door, on the floor next to the others.

The teacher was nowhere in sight, but I didn't have long to wait before I saw her. Two big boys, after huddling together, approached me with a proposal. They promised that if I would yell very loudly into a small screened opening in the schoolhouse wall, a funny thing would happen. Eager to please, filled with curiosity, and well equipped with powerful lungs, I let forth with my mightiest blast. The ventilator led inside to the area where the teacher was hard at work on the first week's assignments, and within seconds she appeared in the doorway looking very disturbed. After threatening loud warnings against any similar performances, she returned to the schoolroom. I was red-faced and grateful that she hadn't asked who'd done it. My education had already begun, and I realized it would take place in the schoolyard as well as inside the building. The yelling trick, I learned later, was a sort of school initiation, one we would use regularly on new classmates and new teachers in the succeeding years.

Before I could reflect on it further, someone suggested a game of Prisoner's Base, and two of the big boys started to choose sides. One took the broom that stood in the school entryway and drew a line in the dirt between the school-house steps and the road. He indicated that a certain fence-post on one side would be one goal, and the nearest swingpole on the opposite side would be the other. I was the last player chosen and, because I had no idea what I was doing, ran around aimlessly, trying to imitate the others. To my chagrin I was quickly captured by the "enemy," taken to the "prison," and told to stay there until someone rescued me. Since my side saw no value in braving the opponents' defenses to save me, there I stayed, disliking school more by the minute.

Finally the teacher again came out of the front door and vigorously rang a shiny brass hand bell. Everyone stopped playing, and I, freed at last, ran to join them in a single line facing the flag. All the children put their right hands above their eyes, palms down, and said in unison, "I pledge allegiance. . . ." At the words "to the flag," everyone extended his hand, pointed in the direction of the flag, palm up and fingers out, still tight together with the thumb inside. I didn't know this ritual and so imitated the others as best I could, mumbling along with them something about invisible Republicans. No one attempted to teach me the words, so it was weeks before I said them in the right order, and even longer before I consistently stuck out the right hand.

Following the salute to the flag, we all filed, in a line led by the teacher, into the building. The older boys and girls took advantage of their seniority and jostled to get the coveted back seats as the teacher refered their selections. There was ample room for us all in the four rows of desks, each with a seat attached. The seats were all the same size—medium, which was much too big for me, and very cramped for the boys and girls nearing sixteen. The seat portion could be folded up, as I became aware when one boy tipped his up and let it fall with a loud bang, causing an instant reaction from the teacher, just as he knew it would.

As the only first-grader, I shared the front row with a girl from the third grade and two second-grade boys, one of them a repeater held over from the year before. In front of each of our desks was an empty seat with no desk, and I soon found out that the pupils went to those four front seats at various times when each lesson was taught.

As soon as we were settled to Miss Anderson's satisfaction the morning exercises, an integral part of each school day, continued. She greeted us and read a short passage from the Bible. We repeated the Lord's Prayer, which fortunately I had learned in Sunday school. Then everyone but me sang the first verse of "America" while the teacher played a very old and wheezy pump organ. "My country 'tis of thee, sweet land of liberty"—the words made no sense to me.

Teacher, as we all called Miss Anderson, next checked off everyone's name in a large black book, the Register. I soon learned that everyone had great respect for that terrifying object. It apparently contained not only our attendance record but also notes about our grades, our behavior, and everything else anyone knew about us. We were all certain that it would very likely be used one day to turn us over to the truant officer, constable, game warden, judge, or whoever else might collect and dispose of bad boys and girls.

During Teacher's attendance check, I looked over the room that I was, according to my mother, destined to occupy for the next eight years. I found under my desk a shelf space for books and papers and was soon to learn that they must be packed in precisely or they would fall into my small lap and onto the floor. On top of the desk was an indented slot for a pencil, and a hole that had once held an inkwell, an item that was now obsolete. Innumerable initials were penciled deep into the wood, and I looked them over carefully, wondering if my father or grandfather had used the same desk.

The room seemed as enormous as a barn to me, although

it was actually no more than twenty-five feet square. The ceiling was very high, since it had been built according to schoolhouse tradition, and there were three small windows on the southeast side and four large ones along the northwest wall. In later years, I suspected that they had been placed in those positions by some diabolical carpenter in order to catch as little winter sunlight and as much north wind as possible. Probably the design was never questioned, since New Englanders did not expect to be comfortable in the winter and had little interest in making their offspring cozy either.

Teacher's big oak desk, with a row of books on top, dominated the front of the room. Behind it was her rickety old brown chair, which could be folded ingeniously into a step ladder. The organ was on the left in front of us, and near it a globe with very faded colors hung from the ceiling on a cord suspended by two pulleys. This fascinating object could be lowered for a closer look by raising a heavy iron ball at the other end of the cord. A few weeks later I discovered painfully that this miniature world could easily be dropped on someone's head if he carelessly loitered beneath it when Teacher wasn't looking. Three large blackboards nearly covered the front wall.

On the right side of the entrance was a sturdy table, painted green and made of wide planks. A metal washbasin, a soap dish, and a white china water jug with blue stripes sat on one end of it. The jug had a little valve at the bottom for drawing off water, and near it were two dozen tin drinking cups, each numbered. A wide drawer in the long table held scrap paper. A pencil sharpener barely out of my reach was fastened to the wall, and a metal wastebasket was beneath the table.

On the other side of the entrance stood a hardwood cupboard with warped doors that could never completely close. It contained our limited supply of lined writing paper, the cheap newsprint paper we used for arithmetic, and the twenty to thirty beat-up books and dictionaries that made up the school library. A large cardboard box in the bottom of the cupboard was filled with paste, scissors, crayons, bottles of ink, dip pens, and blotters.

The most important object in the room was the large clock facing us on the front wall, just above the blackboard. It had the word "Regulator" printed on the glass in front of its swinging pendulum, and in spite of the Roman numerals on the octagonal face, we all learned to tell time long before we learned how to figure. Each child knew at any given time how many more long minutes remained until recess, noon, or quitting time.

To the left of the clock, George Washington stared sternly at each of us from his large framed picture, seeming to disapprove of every move we made or planned to make. Completing the decor, on the other side was a painting of a clipper ship, listing badly on a stormy green sea; and near it hung a calendar from the village general store with the month of June still displayed. I was completely unaware that our schoolroom and its furnishings were an almost exact replica of hundreds throughout the country.

Her attendance check completed, Miss Anderson spent the next half hour rationing out our books, pencils, rulers, and erasers and introducing our courses for the year. Most of the pupils, as we were called—"student" was apparently much too optimistic—received a stack of history, geography, health, spelling, reading, and arithmetic books. I felt cheated because I received only a pencil, an eraser, and one reading book—that was because the first-grade lessons in arithmetic and spelling were made up each day on the blackboard.

Teacher did not waste time reviewing the school rules, since apparently everyone already knew them—except me. This decision on her part turned out to be my bad luck, and I discovered several times during the first week of school that ignorance of the law was not considered an excuse.

I didn't dare to turn around that morning to inspect the person in back of me. The chance to look over my classmates had to wait until morning recess at 10:30. Our ages ranged from my innocent, barely six years to Allen Ritterbush's impressive fifteen. Allen was a giant, six-feet-tall backwoods boy who helped his father cut lumber, trap furs, and make cedar oil. I discovered later that he often carried knives, shotgun shells, and occasionally a small revolver in his pocket; this last item he proudly showed off to the boys and occasionally let us touch. When he quit school on his sixteenth birthday, just before Christmas, we all missed him.

During morning recess, my education in the strange ways of school continued when two older girls asked me to take off my short pants and underwear. Thinking this was probably another strange school custom, I agreeably obliged and was met by shrieks of girlish laughter. Although I was humiliated, the experience left me considerably wiser and less inclined to willingly furnish entertainment for my superiors.

After recess, we lined up to march into school again, and classes resumed. It was then I noticed that the third-grader next to me held up her hand with one finger pointing straight up. The teacher nodded her head, and Lucy went quickly to the pencil sharpener. I was puzzled. How did Teacher know what she wanted? Later I noticed other pupils holding up from one to five fingers. Before noon, I had figured out that these were signals. One finger meant you wanted to sharpen a pencil. Two meant a need to leave the room. ("Toilet" was a bad word, as were all the synonyms—none was ever mentioned during school hours.) Three fingers meant that you needed to get some paper, and four indicated you wanted to whisper to someone, presumably about your schoolwork. Five signified that you were asking the teacher for some help.

By late morning I had experienced all the school I felt I would ever want, and if it had been possible, I'd have written out a resignation on the spot. I was getting powerful hungry, too. When twelve o'clock finally came and Teacher announced that it was noon, we all rushed toward the spot where we'd stacked our lunch boxes. She reminded us that we should wash our hands first, so we grudgingly lined up at the tin wash basin.

We ate in the front yard. Some sat on the cement steps,

others on the ground or in the swings. A few big boys went across the road into a little fortress they had built in previous years among some cherry bushes that grew around a stone wall. Several children sitting near me on the ground swapped sandwiches, but I didn't feel quite ready for that yet, especially since the events of the morning had caused me to be cautious about whom to trust. I hungrily ate everything my mother had put into the box—and in the right order, as she had instructed, except for carefully picking the thick frosting off the cake and eating that first.

The good food reminded me of home, and I felt so much better that I temporarily abandoned my mid-morning plan to run away. I was feeling better, too, because during lunch several children talked to me as if I were one of them and asked me all about myself. When Prisoner's Base resumed, even though I was still the last to be chosen, I found that my small size was a real advantage. I scored some points for my team by being hard to catch. By the third choose-up, I was picked ahead of two of the girls, and my cup began to run over. The games were fun, but I very much wanted to try out the swings and teeter board. Everyone else seemed to prefer playing games, so I didn't have a chance.

After the hour-long lunch period was over, the school bell rang once more, and I was surprised to find there was no line-up or ceremony. Classes started immediately, and I had my first reading lesson. My mother and sisters had already taught me the alphabet and how to read, and the book had a few pictures and looked interesting. The afternoon went much faster.

When Teacher dismissed us at four o'clock, I picked up my empty lunch box for the walk home. Although I knew I still had to face the mean old rooster, I was feeling more grown up after surviving the day at school, and I was sure I'd find some way to outsmart him.

Luck was with me. On the way home, I got a lift with Arnold Rivers, who lived down toward the village. I had seen him when the neighborhood men came in to saw wood during the winter, but he didn't recognize me. "Whose kid be you?" he demanded between chews on his enormous tobacco cud. I told him, helpfully adding a description of where I lived.

"Well, I know you ain't," he said, looking me over accusingly. "I know the Hills, and they hain't got no youn'un anywhere near yer age."

I tried to point out as best I could that I had always been led to believe that I was a Hill, and reluctantly he let me off at our mailbox, still certain I was lying. It had been a long day, and now there was the new worry about where my folks had picked me up.

But for the time being it was a fleeting thought. I was jubilant that I had finally started school, and I was already looking ahead to the day, sometime in the far-off future, when I would occupy a back seat in the classroom.

FIFTEEN-MINUTE WALK—SOMETIMES

My luck at avoiding the Twists' intimidating rooster was short lived. Morning and afternoon, the first week of school, he waited for me, sometimes in the middle of the road, sometimes hidden out of sight, ready to pounce. I tried to outwit him by carrying a big stick, walking backward, and one day even bringing along some corn, hoping to bribe the old red sadist. But none of these tactics worked—he always won, chasing me and jabbing at my legs and arms.

The Twists worked for somebody else and were never at home at the times of day I passed by, so they were of no help. Furthermore, my own family refused to believe that a red-blooded Vermont boy could be bested by a little rooster, so I got no assistance or even sympathy from them.

Fortunately, on Saturday I heard that the old red villain, no doubt heady with his success at bullying me, had tried out his bravado on Mr. Twist. Ralph promptly grabbed his axe and put him on the menu for Sunday dinner. It was a weekend of rejoicing for me, and I walked confidently by their place on Monday morning, unhurried and unbloodied.

The walk to school was a bit less than one mile, and ordinarily took about fifteen minutes. In addition to the Twists' small house, I passed two dairy farms, a clump of woods, a little swamp, and a bridge over a tiny brook. One of the farms was "the Rice place," and Mrs. Rice, in my six-year-old's opinion, was a fine old lady, although she was probably only in her late forties. She was exceptional because she was a free spirit in a neighborhood where one was expected to follow local tradition unswervingly. One of her strange practices was to cultivate a large, fenced-in flower garden that her more practical neighbors described as a "gol' 'ram waste o' land." "Better she spend her time doin' something worthwhile, by crimus," they said. She also had a collection of what seemed to be a million different kinds of cactus plants that filled her entire parlor. "What would she do if someone died and she had to have a funeral in there?" I had overheard the neighbors comment. Parlors were not meant for plants.

One day at school recess, Myrtle Waugh mentioned that Mrs. Rice had not only undergone an operation a few years before, a rare occurrence in our neck of the woods, but she had also survived it, which was rarer still. Myrtle confided in a secretive tone, "She even had her appendix pickled in a jar of alcohol to prove it." This was the pièce de résistance. Previously I had regarded Mrs. Rice with admiration, but at that moment she became a real celebrity. With a fervor that only small children experience, I had a burning curiosity to see the appendix.

Before the end of the second week, I had decided that it would be impossible to walk past the Rice home twice each day without stopping to see that fascinating object. So, Friday afternoon on my way home from school, I marched directly to the front door and boldly knocked. As a somewhat surprised Mrs. Rice peered down at me, I got right to the point without even an "Afternoon, ma'am" or "Nice day, hain't it?"

"Mrs. Rice," I said, "I would like to see your appendix." If the dear woman was somewhat surprised, she didn't show it. She graciously invited me into her parlor, filled to overflowing with cacti, and went to a large bookcase. She took out a small glass bottle and handed it to me. Inside, a strange object slithered around in a clear liquid. I gazed at it for a short time, then thanked her and handed it back, somewhat disappointed. I had expected something more spectacular, like a shrunken head. She probably sensed my letdown and asked me to sit down in the kitchen. As she handed me a freshly baked ginger cookie, my spirits revived. She proceeded to give me such a vivid account of her operation that I felt mighty good about having stopped in and hung on every word, planning to relate each detail later on at home.

Over the supper table, however, my colorful description of the appendix and its separation from Mrs. Rice was not received nearly as well as I had expected. In fact, everyone seemed to be in a state of shock. My embarrassed mother, when she recovered, lectured me sternly. "Small boys," she said firmly, "do not go into homes of people they hardly know and ask if they can view an appendix." She added that she had not included that particular warning on her long list of previous dos and don'ts because she had not anticipated that it was likely to happen.

Monday at school, however, the reaction to my adventure was quite different. My schoolmates were thrilled with my tale, since over the weekend both the drama of the operation and the contents of the bottle had expanded considerably.

Most of my walks to and from school were less eventful, but to my six-year-old's curiosity, they were never dull. Every morning Ma hustled me off at half past eight in the hope I could make the trip quickly enough to have a few minutes to spare. With her warnings about the consequences ringing in my ears, I was never actually late, although occasionally a hundred-yard dash was necessary so I could stand in line for the pledge of allegiance.

All along the way were fascinating phenomena to examine. In the fall, just over the split-rail fence that bordered my route, the old apple trees beckoned, and each week different kinds ripened. From the early Tetoskys, through the mushy Yellow Transparents, dry Wealthies, red Astrachans, and giant Wolf Rivers to the hard, late-maturing Bethels and sugary Pound Sweets, the fruit of each tree needed sampling, as did the red and purple plums.

I tested the red chokecherries, too, to see if by chance some were less puckery than others. It was imperative that I grab the hazelnuts and beechnuts near the stone walls the instant they ripened, too, or the squirrels would get them first, and often they stopped their busy activity to scold me for stealing their food. The woodpeckers, however, always ignored me completely, and no matter how loud I yelled to them, they continued their noisy pounding, often only a few feet away. Geese squawked loudly as they flew southward in big V formations beneath the clear blue autumn sky, and many unfamiliar birds stopped along the roadside on their flights south from Canada.

Occasionally I glimpsed a weasel darting through the crackling dry leaves, or a frightened rabbit dashing across the road. Sometimes a long-legged blue heron fished in the stream, or a giant kingfisher roosted in a tree above, awaiting his prey. Small fish swam noiselessly in the quiet pools, and I usually tossed a few stones into the brook as I crossed the bridge. Sometimes, carefully listening for the troll, I walked down to the water's edge to inspect a few of the brightly colored pebbles, polished smooth by centuries of running water. On most treks to and from school I discovered an assortment of colorful bugs, lizards, toads, butterflies, and other wild creatures that are close to a short boy's head. On rare occasions, I saw a hawk circling overhead, or a deer, fox, or raccoon running across the fields. One morning, an owl that had decided to stay up late blinked at me sleepily from a dead tree stump.

I had been carefully conditioned by the Thornton W. Burgess animal books about all the kindly animal folks and loved the tales of Uncle Wiggly, the nice old gentleman rabbit who wore a high silk hat. The possibility that rabbits would eat up gardens, or that foxes would kill chickens, or deer consume everything from strawberry plants to apple trees didn't occur to me. Any wild creature was my friend.

The walk was not always without concerns. Howls, screams, and other puzzling noises in the woods, or deep rolls of thunder in the west, occasionally warned me to stop loitering and walk faster. Sometimes a mean-looking bull bellowed threats from behind a frail fence, and more than once a herd of unfamiliar cattle broke through someone's fence and filled the road ahead of me.

In winter the days were often snowy and dark, and sometimes very cold and windy, so I had to hurry to keep warm. Deep snow buried the rocks, leaves, and even the stream where I had loitered in the fall, so there was little temptation to linger. Still, the wind sometimes whipped the drifts into strange shapes, some resembling ocean waves; and unfamiliar tracks were often imprinted in the snow. In the soft, glowing, early-morning light, snow crystals sparkled like icy diamonds in the clear air, and now and then mysterious, rainbow-like phenomena we called sun dogs shone on each side of the rising sun.

It was often difficult to walk along the roads when they were freshly covered with fluffy snow, so many mornings I jumped over the fences and stone walls and scampered along the top of the wind-swept frozen snow as the squirrels and rabbits did. Later in the season, when early spring thaws melted the snow into cascades of water that turned the roads into muddy streams, I waded through it, splashing happily in my shiny new rubber boots.

With spring, the temptation to walk more slowly began again. Each day more seeds had sprouted, and by early May there were violets, adder tongues, nosebleeds, and mayflowers to pick and bring home or take to school. New birds were returning from the south each day, and newborn calves and colts tottered in the fields beside their mothers. The brook that had been hidden and tranquil under its icy coverlet and drifts of snow all winter now surged in a river-like current as the deep snows melted in the woods and faraway hills, and some days the waters nearly reached the bottom of the bridge.

Mostly I didn't meet anyone else walking as I trudged along, but occasionally hunters, trappers, and teenagers who were out of school came by, and once I met a clock tinker on his bicycle. Several times I saw the leathery-skinned game warden in his gray uniform, which included a big hat, a badge, and a gun. In my high imagination he always looked as if he suspected I had some illegal fish in my pocket and was debating whether or not to arrest me on the spot. Sometimes the town workmen smoothed the road with a big machine drawn by four horses, or a neighbor passed me enroute to town for provisions or to have his horses shod.

Meeting anyone who was driving a car could be a dangerous experience. I had been warned to always get far out of the way of an approaching car, and after encountering a few I understood why. Because the machine age had come late to our neighborhood, many old pelters had not been driving a car for long and thought they were still handling a horse. I soon learned to recognize Mr. Murphy's old Chevrolet, and when he or others who drove from ditch to ditch came along, I quickly climbed the bank and stayed close to the fence to allow them the use of the entire road.

Although the men driving cars seldom slowed down, people walking or driving horses usually stopped to talk. Most were simply being neighborly to a small boy, but some were lonely, because they lived isolated lives and seldom saw anyone other than their family. Those without telephones or radios were often starved for any kind of news. Although I seldom had much information to give them, I had trouble getting away nevertheless, and many times they nearly made me late for school. They didn't seem to understand about the brass bell, the pledge of allegiance, and the sinister black Register.

BOOK LARNIN', SCHOOLYARD LARNIN'

My first reading book described the simple, pleasant adventures of two disgustingly nice children named Billy and Betty. They were growing up in a typical suburb, leading a life that was very puzzling to us in the backwoods. Their Daddy didn't milk cows but instead rode on a bus every day to something called an office, although what he did there was never described. Their Mommy didn't cook, wash milk separators, can peas, or mend socks but took them to the park, the museum, and even to school. On Saturdays they went to the circus and rode a trolley. They saw fire engines, ice cream carts, organ grinders, balloon men, and numerous other things that were as foreign to me and my classmates as gondolas, rickshaws, and spaceships. None of us had ever seen a paved road, a fire truck, a trolley, a motorboat, or a tractor. Nor had we ridden on an elevator, a train, or a bus.

One chapter described Billy and Betty's happy family having a wonderful time walking in the warm summer rain while water ran down the gutter beside them. To us, a gutter was a trench behind the cows in the barn, and although the teacher did her best to explain the difference, we were as confused by it as we were by the other descriptions of Billy and Betty's life in the suburbs.

I didn't mind the difference between their lifestyle and ours, nor did I envy them at all. Even the youngest of us were aware that the Industrial Revolution was late in getting to our region. I did object, however, when the children visited their Grandpa and Grandma's farm "in the country." Grandpa, un-

like any of the farmers I knew, wore chin whiskers and a red
bandana around his neck, and he usually carried a pitchfork.
He drove a pair of oxen, animals none of us had ever seen. He
also raised turkeys, geese, ducks, cows, horses, goats, and
ponies, and he had a hive of bees. Furthermore, he apparently
did nothing all summer but give his grandchildren pony rides
and rides on wagonloads of sweet-smelling hay. Grandma fed
them fresh vegetables, berries, foamy milk, golden butter, and
ripe red apples—delicacies apparently provided by nature
with no effort on the part of either Grandpa or Grandma. I
knew that life on a farm was quite different from that, and as
I read, I got a smug pleasure in thinking that I knew a lot
more about their lives than they did about ours. The well-
meaning writer, no doubt, wanted only to teach us to read,
but he and his colleagues painted a distorted picture of country life that millions of urbanites believed for years.

Our frayed old textbooks had very few pictures, and
none were in color. They were written to teach rather than
to entertain; and little fables, proverbs, and moral lessons
were scattered generously throughout. Good was always re-
warded, evil suitably punished; and it was difficult to miss the
message even if the teacher failed to point it out. Children
who minded their parents, did their lessons, and worked hard
always grew up to be generals, great inventors, or very rich.
Those who transgressed came to a bad end, without exception.

In some stories like those of Horatio Alger, clean-cut
small-town boys went to the city, where they triumphed over
the lazy, dishonest city lads and soon made fortunes. These
boys invariably came back to their hometowns as heroes. We
eagerly lapped up such stories but knew that the endings
were not true. Anyone who had been a success in the city
would not in any way ever become a hero in our neighborhood. "If'n sech a lad thought he was too good for country
life, well, he could just suck alum and drool" as far as we were
concerned.

Our tattered brown-covered geography books were of

preWorld War I vintage. Although Adolf Hitler was already remaking Europe, his adventures were hard to follow on maps that still showed Serbia and the Austro—Hungarian Empire.

The spelling book consisted of lists of words divided into groups thought appropriate for a young brain to learn in an average lesson. Sometimes the older children passed on little tricks to help us with a difficult word. We learned to spell "geography" by chanting, "George Esdon's old grandmother rode a pig home yesterday."

One history book went as far as the election of President Woodrow Wilson, but most stopped with the Spanish— American War. The cutoff point didn't matter much, however, since each year the sixth-graders had so much trouble with the Revolutionary War that they seldom made it past the Civil War before school let out for the summer.

In history class we learned that the Indians, British, Hessians, Mexicans, and Spanish were bad guys. The Americans were always good guys, as were the French, whenever they were helping out the right side—ours. Our history lessons consisted mostly of long descriptions of various wars. Explorations, inventions, and social progress were sometimes mentioned, but wars dominated, as did the war heroes—Sir Francis Drake, George Washington, Nathan Hale, (General) Gordon Meade, Ulysses S. Grant, and Teddy Roosevelt. The contributions of Fulton, Edison, Howe, Bell, Marconi, and the Wright brothers were briefly mentioned in the text, but they seldom appeared in our reviews or tests. Most of us never heard of Karl Marx, Nikolai Lenin, or Albert Einstein until the mid-1930s, when I was in the seventh grade and we got our first current event papers. Then the world began to seem very close.

Our teachers invariably tried to make us pronounce words correctly and tone down the thick Yankee accent we used at home and play. They had little success. We dropped off letters on words like "shootin'" and "runnin'," and we added letters where the teachers felt they did not belong, such as "mounting" for "mountain." The letter *r* was especially popular. We said "Cuber" for "Cuba," "Americar" instead of "America," "idear" ("idea"), "warter" ("water"), and "barth" ("bath"), and we often spelled them the way we pronounced them.

When we were not reading, our colloquial language was filled with downright bad grammar, and the past tense was especially troublesome: "I brung my little brother to school yesterday." "My older brother had a fight with my father today, and they fit all mornin'." "One of my chores last summer was to keep the garden wed." "We et supper at six o'clock last night." "He run to the woods yesterday." And on and on. "So be you" was a common retort if someone said you were an ignoramus, and we were always free with such phrases as "so don't I," "I weren't," and "he don't." "Ain'ts," "hain'ts," and "'tain'ts" were generously sprinkled throughout everyone's conversation.

It was often difficult to relate our lessons to our lives, because the authors of our texts never included any information about northern New England. We learned far more about South America and Japan than we did about our own region. We lived in a part of the country rich in natural resources and unusual geology; our woods and open hillsides contained an exceptional variety of birds, alpine plants, wildflowers, ferns, mosses, shrubs, and trees, many not commonly found elsewhere. But neither our teachers nor our textbooks were informed, so if any of us discovered such things it was by accident.

One teacher tried to help us understand the importance of conservation and read from our geography book about erosion. "Trees are the best control against erosion," she said. "Try to get your families to plant trees wherever they can, in order to save the soil."

We listened suspiciously. The idea was startling, since we were only a few generations away from the pioneers who had cleared our area. Poplars, wild cherries, and evergreens grew so vigorously all around us that every farmer devoted a great deal of his time to cutting the little seedlings from the pastures, roadsides, and stone walls. The North Woods impatiently waited for an opportunity to once again take over any lands cleared by man, and to us planting trees made about as much sense as sowing dandelion seed.

Memorization had not gone out of style as a teaching tool, and in addition to the proverbs, we were made to learn a variety of poems and passages, including the preamble to the Constitution and the opening paragraph of the Declaration of Independence. We always read aloud classics about such characters as Evangeline, Hiawatha, and the Highwayman, and, because we heard them over and over each year as every class read them, many became forever etched into our memories.

Occasionally a teacher brought in newspapers and magazines for us to look at on wintry days. Most of us devoured every page. *National Geographic* supplied startling photographs of naked natives in Borneo as well as volcanoes, caves, sea monsters, and other exciting things. In addition, each year twenty or thirty books were sent from the state library in a big wooden crate. We met Dr. Dolittle, Anne of Green Gables, Robinson Crusoe, and Kim through them, and most of us read every book at least once and sometimes more. They were the only schoolbooks we ever took home, and they gave us a glimpse into the lives of millions of people who lived beyond the mountain ridge that stood like a giant wall in front of our school.

Having learned to read at home had been a real advantage for me, so by October, Miss Anderson decided it would be easier for me to be in the second grade. This was quite unusual; ordinarily no one was allowed to pass to another grade until he had met a stiff set of requirements. There seemed to be no rush to push a child through school just to keep him with his age group. Aaron Jillson was in the second grade when I started, and in the sixth when I graduated. The dedication of our teachers and the policy of the state Education Department made certain that everyone could read and write before leaving District School No. 9.

My classmates and I never gave it any thought, but our teacher had to be extremely organized and in firm control every minute. She started school at nine each morning and sent us home precisely at four o'clock. In between she taught eight grades, with at least five classes in each, and fitted in two fifteen-minute recesses and an hour for lunch at noon. She also reminded us to take off our caps, pick up our feet when we walked, shut the door, and keep quiet. She was expected to keep the wood stove working, stop all major fights, tie shoelaces, repair broken books and seats, bandage cuts, sweep the floor, listen to the problems the children had at home, and see that we left at four with all our clothes and lunch boxes.

The teacher's schedule demanded that most of our learning be done on our own. Since she could spend only a few minutes with each class, there was no time for lectures or elaborate visual aids. We were expected to do the assigned arithmetic problems and to read our own lessons. Classes were held only to be sure we were doing as instructed. When we were called to the front of the room to recite, we read aloud, answered questions about our assignments, and figured our arithmetic on the blackboard. Occasionally she gave written tests or had us write stories.

Having eight grades in the same room assured that all but the most dense of us learned our lessons well. I heard the sixth-grade history lesson four times before it was actually my turn, once when it was, and twice more before I got out of school. The continual drone of reciting, reading, spelling, and testing also forced us to concentrate, although it was difficult to struggle with my addition and subtraction when the seventh grade was discussing the exciting adventures of John Smith and his first encounter with the Indians. Homework was rarely assigned. Apparently five-and-a-half hours were deemed enough for a child to absorb all the larnin' a body could; and besides, at home one had chores to do.

Although we learned a great deal from books and teachers, we picked up more fascinating knowledge at recess and lunch hour. Each of us contributed heaps of information and misinformation to these sessions. Often our conversation consisted of things we had heard and misunderstood at home, but a lot of youthful imagination was passed on as absolute fact.

We speculated about natural phenomena: "Clouds are really steam created by the sun boiling water in a large kettle." No one seemed to know where such a kettle might be found. "Northern lights are caused by the sun shining on the smooth reflective ice at the North Pole." Someone pointed out that it was dark up there all winter, so it was decided that maybe the moon caused the northern lights. To some children the origin of lightning was a battle in the sky in which the angels hurled thunderbolts. To others, it was God reminding His sinful people that He still was boss. "Sunbeams are the sun drawing up water," presumably to boil and make more clouds. "Trees don't grow all year; they only grow in the summer, except never on Sundays, because nothing grows on a Sunday." "Doctors don't bring babies in their little bag, and yes, girls can have them even if they are not married." "Kittens are born through their mother's mouth." This one brought forth a loud argument since most of us were being raised on farms and had dozens of cats.

We were intrigued by the workings of the human body, a subject that always generated much discussion, usually in groups divided by gender. Since in hygiene class such exciting facts were never mentioned, we were left to our own speculations at recess. I learned that a cut on the hand between the thumb and forefinger would never heal, and in time it would probably kill you. This lore was repeated over and over, and we all believed it fearfully. Having warts meant that you'd touched a toad or that someone had put a curse on you. Playing with certain forbidden parts of your body would make you go blind or crazy—more likely, both. That information made us uncomfortable, too. If you were falling in a dream and didn't wake up before you hit the ground, you would die. We all knew hiccoughs were dangerous, because if you had them for more than a few minutes you could choke to death. They could be cured only by a good scare, and volunteers were always ready to prevent that particular disaster.

Foster Temple, who lived with eight younger brothers and sisters in a tarpaper shack up by Paine Brook for two or three years, kept us spellbound one entire noon hour as he described his newest baby sister's home birth, which he had witnessed at close range.

Frostbite and chilblain were ever-present dangers during our severe winters. The latter always confused Rose Barker, and during each cold snap she insisted on warning us about "chillbrains." She maintained that her family knew someone in New Hampshire who froze his head one winter and promptly got chillbrains. Even after his gray matter had thawed out, he apparently never regained his sanity.

Although sorting out the real and imaginary is always part of growing up, it was more difficult in our community, because it was never easy to obtain the facts from either our books or from uncommunicative families. It seemed that the adults deliberately tried to confuse us, but we suspected that often they didn't know the truth either.

PARTY LINE

During my first year of school, much of the news that circulated originated with Molly Forge and Martha Lincoln, who had telephones in their homes. Near the end of my second year, however, they lost their status as reporters when four more families, including my own, installed telephones. I watched with great fascination as the men with sharp prongs on their legs climbed the tall cedar poles near our house, strung wires, and put a phone in our dining room. Suddenly we were swept into the twentieth century as the humming steel wires connected us with our neighbors and the outside world.

Few people in our area had radios, and those lucky enough to own one were frequently unable to hear anything clearly because reception was so overpowered by static. WGY in Schenectady and KDKA in Pittsburgh were the only stations with strong signals, and they never carried any Vermont news. Although a few families took the county weekly newspaper, for local "doin's" we depended mostly on the phone.

The "telly-phone," as it was pronounced, hung on the wall. It was an oak-colored wooden box about two feet high and one foot wide, with two bells and a mouthpiece in front. The receiver earphone hung on the left side and was connected to the box by a long cord. On the right was a small metal crank. The first day I was left alone in the house, I located a screwdriver and opened the front, the way I had seen the telephone man do. Inside, several thick horseshoe magnets made up the generator. They were activated by the crank, which rang the bells all along the line. Among the other parts were three tall dry-cell batteries that, we later learned, had to be changed by the repairman once or twice a year, depending on how much we used the apparatus.

A telephone subscriber was called a "party," and each of the parties on our line had a different set of signal rings. Every call in or out could be heard by the other nine families. The Forges' ring was three longs and two shorts, the Cheevers' was one long and three short, and ours was a short and a long. An extra-long ring alerted the entire neighborhood to a fire or other emergency, and everyone answered.

It took only a few weeks before we could guess rather accurately by the time of day and the way they cranked the phone who was calling whom. We also knew whether or not the call was worth a listen.

One ordinary long ring got us "Central." All calls to people outside our line went through the operator, Mrs. Luella Gilfillen, in the village. The switchboard was in a little room just off her kitchen, and we heard that her bed was in the same room so that she could wake quickly if there was an emergency at night or if old Lolly Carter got lonely and decided to call her daughter over in Hardwick.

Many people didn't bother to give Central the numbers they wanted. Instead of saying "Five ring twenty-two," which meant number twenty-two on line five, they would say, "Lu, I'd be much obliged if you'd ring up Ed Hawkins." Luella knew everyone's number.

She knew a great deal else, too. "They're not there," she'd tell callers. "They have gone to St. Johnsbury to see the doctor and won't be back until four o'clock." Or, "You'll have to wait a while. I just saw him go to the post office." Not only did she know everything we told her and what she saw, but we all knew that when she wasn't ringing numbers or doing her housework, she plugged into the various lines and listened in. But we were grateful for her curiosity. She always knew where the doctor was, where the mailman was stuck in the mud, and most everything else. Sometimes she alerted the entire town to an emergency like a forest fire or when Jack Calderwood's barn roof fell in.

Having a telephone in your home was a luxury, but it also brought certain obligations. Those of us who had one were expected to deliver messages to the ones who did not, and to let others use it for outgoing calls.

Before our phone was installed, anyone in my family who wanted to make a call had to travel to the Cheevers', nearly a mile away. The $18.00 the telephone cost each year had to be considered carefully by most families, since that same amount of money could buy two sets of overalls and a barn frock, with enough left over for 100 pounds of sugar.

We quickly learned that by putting the receiver over the mouthpiece, we could produce a piercing sound in the ears of everyone listening on the line. This was known as "squawking" and was occasionally used as a protest when someone picked up the phone and overheard some of the neighbors discussing him in an unfavorable way.

Listening in to someone else's conversation was called "rubbering," and everybody did it, although nearly all of them pretended they didn't. "Just happened to pick up the phone and overheard ..." was the common excuse. Women rubbered the most, since they spent more time inside the house, but the men seldom missed a chance, either, when they were free. On our line, everyone could depend on at least six or eight listeners whenever they talked with someone.

Suicides in Vermont are said to have dropped sharply when the rural telephone lines were first built. Undeniably, the phone added a lively new dimension to life in the back country. It became our news desk, news analysis, weather station, all-points bulletin, and daily soap opera. We learned not only the who, what, where, and when of all local events, but also the why. We were up-to-date on romances, births, deaths, marriages, sicknesses, and fires. We kept track of how Grammy Johnson's daughter was doing as she tried to make a living in Hartford, Connecticut, and how Beth Lincoln's ailing uncle in Nevada was progressing. We learned by way of the phone about family fracases, reunions, card parties, work bees, and other doin's—those we were not invited to, as well as the ones we were.

The most important daily newscast was the conversation at 8:30 each morning between Mrs. Whiffle and her mother in the village. Her mother went to the store and post office each morning at eight, picked up the doin's and relayed it to Flossie. Flossie, a first-rate investigative reporter herself, described the goings-on in our neighborhood. The rest of the women on the line listened in, and some took notes.

Suspenseful events sometimes kept us on edge for days. One August the hay in Fred Cheever's barn was getting powerfully hot, because he had put it in too wet and it was beginning to ferment. Fred bored a hole in it with a pump log auger and poked in the thermometer he used for cooking maple sugar.

"It's clearn up to sugar cakes already!" he reported excitedly to Hiram Forge.

"If it goes any higher, ring a long ring on the phone and we'll all come a-runnin' and help you toss it out of the barn," said Hiram confidently. We all stayed "on alert" for the fateful ring but heard nothing more. Apparently his hay finally cooled down by itself.

Another time, the Lincoln and Barker babies were due to be born on the same day, and we all worried about how Dr. Buck would handle the crisis. Everyone thoughtfully stayed off the phone as the two families called back and forth and kept the good doctor driving the mile to and fro between their homes. Meanwhile, the whole party line waited, anxiously wondering which child would arrive first. Everyone breathed a sigh of relief when the babies graciously took their turns and Dr. Buck was present for both deliveries.

One fall day, we overheard that Mark Coomer's young son, Robert, had accidentally shot himself in the foot while practicing Tom Mix—style fast draws with an old six-gun. We learned that Robert was bleeding all over the kitchen floor, but the doctor was tending to a pneumonia case in the next town. Grammy Johnson, who'd picked up the phone and heard the news, ran over and within a few minutes had calmly stopped the bleeding until the doctor could arrive. Robert made such a fast recovery, he was ready for the next trapping season and proudly showed everyone the patched-up little hole in his boot.

High melodrama on the party line sometimes made our ears tingle. Robert Kilbourn's daughter Gracie called Froth Hudson's nineteen-year-old son Jack late one night and got right to the point. In a desperate voice she told him that she was going to have his baby, and he just had to marry up with her. Jack listened patiently to her tears and threats, then quietly hung up, packed his valise, and lit out for Massachusetts that same night. He didn't come back for nearly ten years. That call gave the neighborhood plenty to talk about for months.

We could count on more excitement when Art Lyford, from the other side of town, came to his friend's home on our party line to make the calls he didn't want his own neighbors to hear. Each time, he had been fighting with his wife and was calling his lawyer in Newport, the county seat. Usually he had just moved out of his house into the barn and wanted to start divorce proceedings immediately. A few days later, as we all rubbered again, he'd invariably phone his attorney to tell him that they'd patched up their quarrel and decided to call off the whole business. His lively marriage kept us on edge two or three times each year.

Bits of helpful information were generously passed around by phone. We learned that "Davis's Store is paying two cents a dozen more for eggs than Cuthberson's," or "Cole's Store is having a sale on coffee." It appeared that one could be ahead about fifteen cents by driving ten extra miles, which people frequently did, feeling very good about their business sense.

Mrs. Coomer could always be relied upon for an instant analysis of, and comments on, the news. People who are very rich, slightly crazy, or very old can apparently get away with saying just about anything, and Jerusha Coomer qualified for two out of the three. One day someone reported that Jack Cristy's son and daughter-in-law were going to have a baby. "Just a minute, I'll be right back," she said. After a few minutes she announced, "I always write down when people get married, so I went to look it up. They were married on October 3rd. That was ten months ago, so it's all right."

News was so scarce that if we missed an event, we could usually get an instant replay of it any time of the day or evening, as people expanded and commented on the goings-on. No item was too inconsequential for comment. One day Tilly Tootson put a quarter in the mailbox, asking for five three-cent stamps, five penny postcards, and two of the cent-and-a-half stamps used for mailing unsealed greeting cards. Since the regular mailman was not on duty that day, his substitute handled the transaction. Unfortunately, he forgot to put Tilly's one-cent change in the mailbox.

When Tilly noticed that her change was missing, she promptly called the offending mailman on the phone. Thinking she was joking, he laughed uproariously. He learned immediately that it was a mistake to take her comments lightly, as Tilly gave him "what for" and told him she expected to find her one cent in the box the next day. When it wasn't there, she spent the rest of the week calling everybody she knew to tell them about it and even threatened to call James Farley, the postmaster general. Some people considered slipping her a penny just to shut her up, but apparently no one did. We all knew that the next week she'd create a new crisis.

If two women were having a chat and seemed unsure of the facts, often a third and sometimes more would join in. Panel discussions made it possible to cover more subjects, and more people could be talked about. The duration of the conversation was also expanded, thus making it more difficult for anyone wanting to make a call to get the line.

Because the telephone was used constantly for idle chatter, some farmers became very testy when they needed to use it for business and could not get the line. Everyone was willing to yield to someone who had to make a call to the doctor or to report a fire, but most women considered ordinary barn talk no emergency and felt it could just wait a spell.

One day Steely Lincoln came into his house to contact a buyer to pick up a newborn calf. He got more and more "het up" as the chatter went on and on between the Coomer and Waugh households. Miz Coomer knew somebody or other who had a birthday on every day of the year until February 23, and she was going through the entire list that morning. She announced that if she could find a name for that day, she would have a complete list until March 17, if she could count St. Patrick. Mrs. Waugh was sure she knew someone who had come into the world on the twenty-third, but she couldn't recall who it was. "My memory ain't what it used to be. I can't even think. I don't know what to say." "Why don't you say goodbye?" yelled the exasperated Mr. Lincoln, who had rubbered through fifteen minutes.

Another time, Fred Cheever was reaching for the phone to call the feed store when Mrs. Lincoln beat him to it. "I've just put a couple of pies in the oven and, by gravy, I thought I'd jaw with you a bit while they're baking," she told a neighbor. Fred hung up the phone, waited a while, and picked it up again. Several listens and ten minutes later there was no indication that the women would ever slow down. Finally he could stand no more.

"I can smell pies burning," he said excitedly into the phone. There was a short scream, and the line was Fred's.

Although Ma Bell helped dispel the loneliness and brought a new way of life to the backwoods, she also caused considerable trouble. Waldo Markres pointed out to his wife that their house was a mess. He threatened to have "the gol' 'ram contraption" taken out if she didn't stop spending three hours every morning with it. Later, we heard Geraldine tearfully telling her listening public that, given the choice, she would rather part with Waldo than the telephone.

People in our neighborhood rarely made long-distance

calls. It was expensive and took far too long, and one had to shout loudly to be heard. If one of our neighbors wanted to call Boston to inquire about cattle or Christmas tree prices, the operator first called St. Johnsbury. That operator, in turn, called the one in White River, who called the next big town, and so on along the line until, ten minutes later, they finally reached their party in Boston. When the connection was made the static was usually so loud it was a struggle to hear accurately what was being said.

When many receivers were off the hook, the power was drained from the battery-powered voice box of the caller. Everyone listening in on a long-distance call had to make a decision about whether to hang up and make it easier for the caller to hear and be heard, or to hang on and not miss the exciting news. Occasionally a caller couldn't hear his party at all and begged everyone to hang up. One time Jean Lapointe yelled in his thick French accent: "I call you all back and tell you about it later!" He did, too.

All Western Union telegrams were delivered by phone. They usually told of the demise of a relative who lived so far away that no one could go to the funeral anyway, so a post card could have brought the information just as well. Still, the telegram was so connected with death that most families felt it was the proper way to convey the news, and we all did it.

Generally, everyone accepted "listening in" as a way of telephone life and recognized that there was nothing they could do about it. Codes were developed among friends, especially the girls, so others wouldn't recognize the important secrets they were passing along. Annie Markres and Helen Lapointe learned pig Latin and tried it out occasionally, but it fooled only a few people, and the rest figured it out easily. Most of line three seemed to feel that it was probably better to have the neighbors know exactly what was happening rather than imagine something worse.

Hiram Forge once wound up his conversation about millet seed with John Barker by saying, "Well, goodbye, John; goodbye, Miz Cheever; goodbye, Miz Coomer; goodbye,

Hanna; goodbye, Tilly; goodbye, Miz Rice; goodbye, Miz Hill; goodbye, Miz Waugh."

So ingrained became the telephone-listening habit that if we were visiting someone and the phone rang, our hostess might absent-mindedly leave us and go to listen in. Sheepishly, she would quickly return and mumble some excuse like, "I thought that was my ring" or "I expected my sister to call." Later on, when the lines were split up and there were only three or four households on each circuit, most people had the feeling they were missing out on something.

When Sam Traverse sold his farm and retired to the village, he announced happily to all his former neighbors that he planned to spend a lot of his new free time rubbering on the telephone. He was furious when he found that the phone company had installed a private line.

BLACK CATS AND HORSE HAIRS

Although it signaled the approach of a long, hard winter, October was an exciting month of change. Bright orange, crimson, and yellow leaves shone against the brilliant blue sky, and the clear fresh air was so refreshing and invigorating that even an active schoolboy could not ignore the season.

By October the days had become so short that it was dusky when we started home from school at four o'clock, and life began to move more slowly on the farm, too.

We let the cattle outside only during the day, because of the frosty nights, and I marveled at the giant harvest moon as it rolled silently over the distant mountain and showered the dark, leafless trees with a spooky, golden light.

We needed to dig our warm winter sweaters, mittens, and wool touques out of storage for the morning walk to school, and these made the clothing corner in the schoolroom smell of a rich mixture of mothballs and cedar boughs.

We played less vigorously at recess, and we talked more. The stories became more frightening as we approached the scariest, most superstition-ridden night of the year and our imaginations soared. We tried to outdo one another with supernatural tales, and at night we spotted headless horsemen and sheeted ghosts around every corner.

Halloween always accentuated the natural bent of our neighborhood to believe in superstitions. Everyone I knew, young and old, had beliefs that made them cautious and uncomfortable. The number 13 was considered especially risky. I found even being 13 years of age unpleasant. Friday was equally fateful, and no intelligent Yankee had ever been known to start a project on that day. A man who needed to begin plowing a field on Friday would go out on Thursday evening, sometimes very late, and plow one furrow to ensure that no disaster would subsequently happen. Many stories circulated of barns that burned or collapsed, legs that were broken, and crops that failed simply because they involved something that had commenced on a Friday. I heard over and over that the main reason the Snortles' marriage had broken up—a rare occurrence in our hills—was that they had been wed on a Friday evening.

We all knew people who would turn around and return home if a black cat crossed in front of them, even if they had already traveled many miles. At one time the Lapointes had several black tomcats on their farm, and Mark Coomer refused to drive by there because he felt it risky. Unfortunately for us all, the cats were very active and circulated freely around the neighborhood on early spring nights, and soon there were black cats everywhere. Even though he had a choice of several roads, poor Mark was hard pressed to find a route into town that didn't start him off wrong.

Froth Hudson stoutly maintained that a cat's fur had to be entirely coal black in order for it to be unlucky, and he pointed out that most local felines had a few white hairs under their chins. Mark and his neighbors were not convinced, however, and were not about to take a chance.

Black cats only headed the list of happenings to worry about. If we were to spill the salt, raise an umbrella in the house, or drop a dish towel, it meant bad luck and possibly even death. Allowing a rocking chair to rock with no one in it signaled that one of the family or close acquaintances would die shortly. Even lame or elderly people would painfully rise to quickly stop a moving chair if a person or a cat had gotten out of it and left it rocking. Breaking a mirror somehow messed up your soul and undoubtedly resulted in seven years of bad luck. The ill fortune resulting from all these acts was not a remote possibility, or idle speculation, but an absolute fact. When any of them happened, as they often did, we knew that inevitable catastrophe lay ahead.

My family believed that we should be aware of other signs, too. A dog howling near a house at night also meant an upcoming death. If someone died on a Friday or Saturday and lay unburied over Sunday, two more deaths would occur soon. Actually, we expected that all tragedies would come in threes, and no one quite relaxed until the third event had taken place—even if it were months later, and it took quite a bit of imagination to link it up with the first two.

There were many superstitions regarding food. Dropping a fork meant that company would be coming. If we were to take a second helping of potatoes while we still had some left on our plate, someone always predicted that a person more hungry than we were would drop in during the day. Every housewife believed that food from a tin can had to be removed immediately after opening, or it would become deadly poison within a few seconds. My mother always ran across the room to dump the contents immediately.

Finding one's true love was also fraught with strange beliefs. Sometimes a single girl would pare an apple, take the entire peeling off in one piece, and throw it over her right shoulder. Supposedly it would form the initial of her future husband. Others would walk down stairs backward, carrying a candle in one hand and looking in a mirror held in the other. Their mate-to-be was supposed to appear in the mirror.

Many folks believed that if you took a bath or even washed your hair without waiting an hour after eating, you could get a stomach cramp and die. Some were sure that salt thrown over the left shoulder would counteract a threatened disaster of this or any other sort, but only if it were done promptly.

Tall tales passed around at school recess also gave me cause for concern. If anyone swallowed an apple seed, it was likely to sprout somewhere inside, and soon tree limbs would grow out of both nostrils. "Honest, it happened to a girl in St. Johnsbury just two years ago," said Rose Barker. She and her sister Lily were our school authorities on such matters. Many times I heard that if we swallowed chewing gum, it would stick somewhere in our interior and promptly cause appendicitis.

One gloomy October day, Lily and Rose announced with great authority that snakes spring to life from bits of horse hair: "Our uncle told us, so there." Although some of us expressed doubt, Rose was unyielding. "Horse hairs fall into brooks and puddles," she said, "and after a few days they turn into little snakes."

The Barker girls always talked in an excited "you'll never believe this, but it's the gospel truth" manner. I knew that most of their stories were inaccurate, but even so, this particular origin of little reptiles was disturbing to my fertile nine-year-old mind.

One of my jobs on the farm was to water the horses, so I often saw their hair in and around the tub. I was concerned about the possibility of a major snake invasion the next summer, especially since the tub was very close to our house. Like most country folks, I disliked and feared snakes, especially since I went barefoot a lot. Although Rose's theory went against the laws of biology as I understood them, I gathered a lot of horse hairs one day and put them in a bucket of water. I checked them carefully every day, watching for motion or any change of size or color. Weeks later, when they were still soggy hairs, I confronted Rose with my findings.

"Probably you did something wrong," she said, closing the matter. The snake story had been told weeks before. That day she was excited about fallen angels and could handle only one excitement at a time.

"My cousin Jody, over in Albany, saw an angel fall right out of the sky one night," she announced. "It was behind his house, and their barn burned down that very night." I resolved not to be alarmed. She had been wrong about snakes, so she was probably wrong about angels. I told her and everyone else how I felt, but no one listened. Rose could be most convincing, and she always knew someone who knew someone to whom these momentous things had happened. So for a long time afterward, in spite of my bravado, I kept one eye on the night sky for fallen angels, just in case, and probably some of the other kids did, too.

The girls weren't the only ones who brought in tales of horror. David Finney's uncle passed along some Sunday editions of Boston newspapers that David brought to school. These were alive with stories about lost spirits, Egyptian curses, haunted houses, and gypsy rituals. David's Uncle Herman became our most respected source of information on such subjects, as well as of prophecies of coming disasters (such as the end of the world), always quoting someone who had never been wrong before.

Roberta Ritterbush knew of a man who had suddenly burst into flames while eating dinner with his family one day. "Spontaneous combustion, just like hay heating," she claimed. Kate Hudson had a cousin who lived for a time in a house in Ware, Massachusetts, where a man with no face wandered through the rooms occasionally. Someone else told us of a house where Revolutionary War music could be heard in the walls on cold winter nights.

"They must be very old houses," I said, feeling sorry that ours was only a century old.

Although my family was superstitious, their beliefs were founded on those of their ancestors. They pooh-poohed most of the stories I brought home from school, although their disdain didn't discourage me from collecting the tales.

The stories livened up our school life at recess, but like my family, the teachers refused to discuss them with us when we asked for verification. The half hour each day we spent practicing for the upcoming school Halloween program was enough of ghosts and goblins for them.

We actually had two Halloweens each fall. The most important was the one celebrated by our school party and dance, traditionally held some evening during the last week of October. The other, the real Halloween, which came on the last night of the month, didn't mean much to us. It existed mostly in hearsay and stories about wild happenings in other places, or way back when the old folks were young. None of us was allowed to go outdoors on that frightening night. "No, you are not going out," we were told. "That way, you won't get the blame if something bad happens."

So, in spite of the threats made by the big kids in school every year, Halloween night was about like every other night in our area. We knew the farmers were heavily armed, and some were rumored to have loaded their shotguns with pellets of rock salt for the occasion. Froth Hudson made it known that anyone foolish enough to be found on his premises on Halloween night would quite likely be found there the next morning.

HALLOWEEN

The Halloween program on the last Friday of October was the biggest event of the school year, and it commanded a far bigger crowd than did the Christmas, Memorial Day, and school picnic celebrations combined. Each neighborhood family always came en masse, with grandparents and with babes in arms.

During my first year at school, I discovered that I was expected only to say a little poem and make my mouth move noiselessly during the songs. I was also doomed to go home with my family as soon as the program was finished—before the fun began. With each passing year, however, a child was allowed more freedom and given more responsibility. By the time I was eleven, I was one of the older children and was expected not only to arrive early on the night of the Halloween program but also to stay until the evening's festivities were over and help put everything back in its place.

That landmark year I was one of three members of the seventh grade. On the Friday afternoon of the big event, instead of having classes, we transformed the schoolroom into a party hall. Our cut-out orange pumpkins, black cats, and witches already covered the walls and windows. The pumpkins we had brought from home were carved with grotesque laughing and frowning faces and were strategically placed on windowsills and tables. We rigged wires, strung up several sheets (borrowed from our parents), and constructed a stage in the front of the room. For extra seating we hauled in the wide wooden planks that were stored in the woodshed for such occasions and set them on chunks of maple firewood.

Although I felt very grown up that evening and was proud to be considered old enough to go early, I did not enjoy walking the familiar mile in the dark for the first time. The wind howled and tossed around the black clouds in a peculiar and frightening way. The moon appeared only occasionally, making spooky shapes of the naked maple trees. Every sound a mouse or weasel made in the dead leaves on the ground was amplified a hundred times in the black night. My lantern was no help because instead of dispelling the gloom, it created frightening dark shadows as I walked, making me clearly visible to all the John Dillingers, Nazi spies, gypsies, and ghosts lurking behind the trees. The mile never seemed longer, and my heart had never pounded harder.

It was a great relief to find Steve already at school. He was the eighth-grader who was acting as janitor that year, and he had unlocked the door and lit the school's single kerosene lamp. If he had been at all scared from his own mile-long hike through deep woods from the other direction, he didn't show it—but he had no way of knowing how terrified I had been, either.

Soon the teacher and several other kids arrived, each carrying a lantern. In the flickering light we lit the candles inside the jack-o'-lanterns and organized the props for our upcoming performance. A twig broom and black kettle stood by for the witch, and several extra sheets awaited the ghosts. We also set up a ticket table. Those over sixteen had to pay twenty cents to get in, unless they brought a box lunch for the box party following the performance.

By working fast, we were almost finished before the audience began to arrive. I lived only a mile from the school, so my family came later, by themselves, but because some of my classmates lived two or three miles away, their parents brought them early and stayed. All their little brothers and sisters came early, too, and persisted in getting in the way of our grown-up activities.

All the early arrivals brought kerosene lamps or lanterns with them, so the schoolroom soon glowed with an unfamiliar brightness. Waldo Markres placed his big new gasoline lantern with twin mantles on a windowsill, where it hummed and whistled. Although it made everyone sitting near it nervous, it flooded not only the room but also part of the schoolyard with a brilliant white light that made all the other lamps look reddish and weak.

Everyone had milked the cows early and had taken an unaccustomed weeknight bath. As people filed in to take seats on the hard plank benches, their spoken greetings were terse. An outsider might have thought the group was either completely unacquainted or the most unfriendly gathering that had ever met under one roof; but it was the Yankee way, the way the Lord intended. A grunted "Yessir," "Yeah," "Evenin'," or "'Lo" were the most common salutations. There were rare "How be ya's?" and an occasional "How's your sick horse a-comin'?" but there was no handshaking or backslapping, and certainly no hugging or kissing. All members of each family sat together, and the Kennisons and Jillsons, who were not speaking to one another that week, made it a point to sit a good distance apart. We were all aware of their little feud, because they scowled frequently at one another and at all those who nodded to the folks they were mad at.

By seven o'clock we had a full house, with the plank benches and school seats overflowing. Small children sat on their mothers' laps, and the older boys stood along the walls to make more room. We schoolboys in knickers and girls in colorful dresses waited impatiently in the wings of the sheet curtains until we were called on. This allowed the teacher to keep an eye on us, and made more room for the audience. Finally Laurie Finney, who lived only a half mile away, arrived last as usual, making our school attendance 100 percent. A hush dropped over the audience, and as Aaron Jillson and Robert Coomer pulled open the sheet curtains, District 9's one-hundredth-and-some-odd annual Halloween celebration got underway.

Nothing ever went smoothly at these events, and no one expected it would, except the hopeful teacher. Usually one cute first-grader was selected to give a welcoming speech intended to put the crowd in a good mood. That year, five of the youngest children shared the honor. Each had memorized a little poem, and they carried large letters to spell out HELLO. As they filtered from the wings to the front with their letters, the child with the o hesitated a few seconds, then ran to the wrong end. Our startled neighbors and parents were greeted with a cheery OHELL.

Although it must have been challenging to produce a play with only five or six children above the fifth grade, our stalwart teachers never stopped trying. That year's production, as usual, was well stocked with frightened girls, witches, a ghost, disappearing people, a grouchy old man, and a goblin or two. Because of the shortage of actors and actresses, though, each older kid had to play two or three parts. It was necessary for some of us boys to change very rapidly from being sheet-clad ghosts or goblins, parts we liked, to girls in sunbonnets, which we did not like. The theatrics must have been confusing to our audience, and probably no one understood for certain what was supposed to be happening. The half dozen pre-schoolers who sat in the front row, only a few inches from the performers, were distracting, too, as they frequently made comments or asked questions that the younger actors in the play agreeably answered.

Miss Reynolds, the director of the bedlam, flitted to and fro, trying to get her actors and actresses on stage and to signal the more enthusiastic players to come off when their speeches were completed. As she became more distraught, we gained confidence, lapping up the applause and enjoying every moment, until we forgot the words to the second verse of the final song. Only Torry Waugh remembered, and he started it completely alone in his high-pitched, changing voice. Everyone laughed, and our cockiness vanished.

Finally, to everyone's great relief, Miss Reynolds announced that the program was over. She thanked the crowd for coming and announced the plans for the rest of the evening. This year was to be different from most years. Usually, following the performance, there was a "fish pond" at which the little children, for a penny or two, could angle for a gaily wrapped, cheap little toy; and a candy table to which the various fudge makers of the neighborhood had donated their wares so that the school could make a little extra money. Sometimes, too, there was a punch bowl from which for three cents we could drink a glass of colored liquid bravely termed "punch." This year, however, there was to be a box party between the show and the evening dance.

The box party was an old country tradition that combined the excitement and competition of an auction, the fun of eating, and the opportunity for some worthwhile organization to make a small profit. The girls and women created fancy boxes decorated with colored paper, ribbons, and homemade flowers, packed them with their best meal, and brought them to the party concealed in brown paper bags. In our neighborhood it was quite likely that the single young ladies would drop a hint or two about the decoration to their favorite boyfriends, since the ladies might have to share the meal with old tobacco-chewing Jim Slicer or toothless John Jacobs if they were the high bidders.

Usually the contents of the boxes were as elegant as their exterior decorations, since no woman wanted to appear incompetent in front of her neighbors. Cinnamon rolls, fried chicken, stuffed eggs, elegant sandwiches, chocolate cake, pie, coffee in a big thermos, cookies, apples, and pieces of fudge were some of the yummies we knew were in that big pile of boxes. All the food was homemade and home-raised. No woman would have even considered putting store-bought bread or cookies in a box, even if they had been affordable (which, of course, they were not).

As usual, cigar-smoking Mark Coomer was our auctioneer. Fat and good-natured, he clowned around as he pushed the prices on the most favored boxes to startling heights. His wife, sitting beside him, recorded the names of the bidders and collected their money in a blue metal tobacco can. Occasionally she had to argue with the young swains who felt they couldn't possibly have bid as high as the figure she had recorded.

A whisper soon spread around the room that Miss Reynolds's box was next to be auctioned. Since she was young, cute, and single, and marrying the schoolteacher was a common local occurrence, competition for her box was especially keen. We were all amazed when several young men who earned less than a dollar a day eagerly pushed the bidding so high that Roger Lincoln's older brother, Jerry, had to pay nearly $2.50 to claim his prize. As a rule, boxes sold for 20 to 40 cents only, and the ones in the pile set aside especially for the children usually brought 5 or 10 cents each.

Most buyers seemed to be satisfied that they had made a good deal, but there were a few disappointments and surprises after the bidding. Wallace Macomber, a middle-aged bachelor, thought he was bidding on the teacher's box and was considerably surprised to find that he had bought Emma Flint's instead. Although Emma lived outside the district, she always went to every Grange and church card party and all the box suppers she heard about. Wallace began to feel consoled when he found that her big box was well stuffed with delicious goodies, until Emma let out a loud yell. Six of her nine children came a-runnin', and they all ate from it, too.

Jack Wallace, whose wife was the best cook in the county, had the misfortune to buy the box put up by Flossie Whiffle, who was probably the worst. Flossie's treat that night was sandwiches made of thick slices of slightly burned bread, generously spread with dark, heavy molasses. Jack was still grumbling when he went home with his lantern, hours later.

Eating seemed to relax the crowd, and the event resembled a big picnic, with neighboring families joking and having fun with one another. For a few minutes the cows, crops, and mortgages that usually dominated their thinking were forgotten.

I debated a long time over whether to spend my only ten cents for a box or to go without supper. Hunger finally won out. I was lucky and ate with my classmate Molly Forge, who had packed a good meal. She was nice, but it was obvious she had been hoping that Conrad Lapointe would buy it instead. Conrad had carefully hung on to his money, however, and never made a bid.

After we ate I ran around with my friends trying to see everything and speculating about how many rules we could get away with breaking. Both Teacher and our parents had warned us to stay inside, not to talk with people we didn't know, and never to accept food, drinks, or smokes from strangers.

During the supper period, many new people from "away" filtered into the room. Most were in their late teens or slightly older. The girls wore heavy eye shadow, lipstick, and very red rouge. They also had high heels, frills on their dresses, and noisy dingle-dangles on their wrists. They talked in shrill voices and giggled incessantly.

At first the boys who accompanied them didn't come into the room but hung around just outside the door, trying to look and talk tough. Unlike the neighborhood men, who were dressed in their best coats, vests, and ties, most of the boys wore tight overall pants with copper rivets, open black vests, and wide belts studded with colored stones. They kept their shirt collars turned up, puffed vigorously on cigarettes, and pretended to ignore the girls until the dancing started.

By the time the last bite of food was gone and Joe Waugh had produced his final loud burp, we had stacked the seats and desks in one corner. People sat on the thick planks placed against the schoolroom walls, waiting patiently for the music makers to finish their tuning up. Wallace Davison had been imported from Sheffield to do the fiddling, and Hattie Gooley, who lived near the village, was to play chords on the school's wheezy old pump organ. Wallace was a bewhiskered old mountain gentleman who looked as if a thought had never crossed his mind during his lifetime, but he knew hundreds of fiddle tunes by heart and could reel them off for hours on end.

Finally Wallace and Hattie seemed satisfied that they

were close enough to the same key, and after a short conference with Steely Lincoln, who called the changes, they swung into the lilting music of "Haste to the Wedding." Most of the older folks paired off to do the Virginia Reel, forming two long columns that stretched from one end of the schoolroom to the other.

Dance followed dance, with at least a dozen and a half couples crowding the tiny floor. Steely, a short little Scottish farmer with an incredible sense of rhythm, danced among them, and in a high-pitched voice he expertly guided everyone through line dances such as "Boston Fancy," quadrilles like "Honolulu Baby," and circle dances like "Soldier's Joy."

During one vigorous dance, Snort Finney's belt came loose and flew across the room. His plump wife, who had been sitting on the sidelines, rescued it, and gave chase as he whirled through the dance. "Never fear, Ella," he called to her loudly, "for I still have on my trusty galluses."

The little children, taking advantage of their parents' preoccupation, wrestled in the corners. We older boys roamed around, enjoying the motion of the dancers inside and curiously exploring the mysterious activities of the nondancers outside. Billy Tootson, who was two years older than I, pointed out that a lot of couples stayed in their cars until after intermission when we stopped charging admission.

"Let's sneak around and see what they're doing in there," he said to Roger and me, indicating the cars parked some distance down the road. I was interested, but Roger was wiser and more cautious. He had heard that some men carried loaded pistols and had once threatened some boys who were snooping around at a school dance in Stannard. Also, he had heard that a man had once thrown a beer bottle at a boy, nearly breaking his leg. So we stayed away from the cars, but as we wandered around close to the building, we heard some loud arguments, lots of squealing and giggling, and the tunes of some songs with strange, unfamiliar words. We were careful to get back inside the schoolroom before we were missed, however, and risked having to go home early.

Certain rituals were strictly observed. After each dance, the married men retired to one corner of the room, the women to another, and the single girls to a third. The unmarried young men retreated outdoors. Most of the school-age children hung around the front of the room near the fiddle player and organist.

Occasionally, to give the caller and square dancers a rest, the little orchestra played a waltz, foxtrot, or polka. Although a few couples glided expertly across the floor, most round dances were attempted only by older girls who danced with each other. The boys seemed reluctant to brave the stares of the older folks and the sneers of their contemporaries and try the unfamiliar steps, at least until they had been fortified by several more drinks.

At eleven o'clock, the music makers took a half hour's rest. Hattie chatted with the women, and Wallace helped himself to a dark liquid in a Coca-Cola bottle, although it had not smelled at all like Coca-Cola when Roger and I investigated it earlier. Most of the older folks went home at intermission time, taking a good number of the lanterns and all the young children with them.

Just as Billy had promised, the couples that had been in their cars began to come in after intermission. They danced with considerable flourish and noise, primed by the booze they'd consumed and feeling brave in the dim light. Since I'd never before been allowed to stay for this part of the evening, I was thrilled to see the lively dancing and hoped to discover some of the sinful things that were alleged to take place.

Fortified by additional nips from his bottle of dark liquid, Wallace fiddled in a more and more peppy manner, and by midnight Hattie decided to let the old guy go it alone. No one seemed to mind. The girls were swung harder, often completely off their feet, and they squealed louder. Once old Johnny Jacobs, toothless and hairless, went out on the floor and did a little jig all by himself as everyone clapped in time to the music. A few new boys came in and, although they didn't dance, stood around the sidelines watching the show, their eyes bleary and their voices thick. They leaned heavily on one another and looked as if they might tip over at any minute.

Another group I hadn't seen before joined the party at about midnight—six or seven young men probably in their mid-twenties, though they looked much older. The whispers went around the room that they were French-Canadian lumberjacks from a nearby camp. They wore red checkered woolen shirts and breeches and high leather boots only partly laced. Most looked surprisingly healthy, compared with the local youths, though they sported long, uncombed hair and beards that varied in age from a few weeks to several months. One was cross-eyed, and another had what I found out later was a harelip.

As we stared at them, they stared back hard and unashamedly. They smelled of an unusual combination of beer, spruce pitch, and chewing tobacco mingled with gasoline and oil, presumably acquired from working on their ancient and very noisy cars. They were a completely new breed to Roger and me, and, burning with youthful curiosity, we tried to find out who they were and where they came from. But they probably understood no English and ignored us completely. In fact, they spoke to no one and only occasionally made strange-sounding grunts to one another that sounded like half laughs and half sneers. They didn't dance, and after a few minutes they left. We followed them out into the bright moonlight, watching their car wheels kick up the dirt and their engines backfire loudly as they tore off into the night.

By one o'clock, when only the school lamp and a few kerosene lanterns were left, Wallace and Hattie teamed up for "Home Sweet Home," the traditional signal that the dance was over. As the song ended, the few remaining dancers left slowly, singing, humming, and whistling as if to prolong the evening by a few more minutes. One of the jeans-clad boys whipped out a harmonica and began to play it with one hand as he danced around, holding a red-lipped girl closely with the other. She giggled, bent far backward, and twirled a long string of beads with her free hand.

The teacher boarded with Snort Finney, so he stayed to take her home. He and Steely Lincoln helped us pick up the empty lunch boxes and papers and carry the heavy planks and chunks back to the woodshed. The teacher paid the musicians, swept the floor, and directed the replacement of the desks and seats and the dismantling of the Halloween decorations. We learned later that Steely returned to the schoolyard early the next morning to pick up the cigarette wrappers, empty beer bottles, and other sinful objects the older youths had discarded so there was no chance that we innocent children would find them on Monday morning.

The golden harvest moon was heading toward the western sky when we said goodbye, still excited by the evening's festivities and thrilled with the money the school had made. We started our separate ways home, each clutching a smoky, flickering lantern.

We all knew that the next day would be a busy Saturday. Time was running out fast before winter would arrive. I would probably help my brothers put block wood into the house shed or stack long sticks of limb-wood in the sugar house for next spring's maple syrup boiling, or perhaps help bank the house with fir boughs or put on the double windows. But tomorrow seemed far in the future. Tonight my head whirled with new sights, smells, and gay fiddle tunes.

The walk home seemed even darker and more frightening than it had been earlier in the evening. I wanted to run all the way, but that was impossible while I carried the bulky kerosene lantern that I fervently hoped would burn for another ten minutes. Each rustle in the dry, frozen leaves made me jump, and the echoes of a hound dog baying miles away sounded like a pack of hungry wolves a few feet up the road.

In the shadowy darkness I remembered vividly the story that Rose and Lily Barker had told us a few days before about a group of people who had completely disappeared off the face of the Earth. They claimed that Fred Lichen, who'd once lived down the road a few miles, had dropped from sight eight or ten years before, and furthermore, Grammy Corkins had heard a scream far above her house that fateful night. The girls, in their usual hushed and excited tones, were sure he had been carried off by demons from another world.

Roger Lincoln told me later that his folks said that Fred had simply deserted his wife and eight children and walked six miles to the railroad station in the village. There he got into an empty boxcar, rode to Burlington, where no one knew him, and then bought a ticket to Manitoba. He also pointed out that Grammy Corkins had been deaf for twenty years and so probably wouldn't hear Gabriel's trumpet in the next room. But even though I knew full well that one should discount 90 percent of everything that was in the Barker girls' newscasts, I was also very sure that a lot of things were possible on an October night that would never take place on a July afternoon.

The safety of our warm house, with its crackling fire and sturdy door, never felt better, and my warm bed never seemed more secure. I quickly drifted off to sleep in a dreamy maze of whirling dancers; perfumed, painted ladies; noisy cars; tasty food; and the lilting strains of "Irish Washerwoman," "Golden Slippers," and "Mrs. MacLeod's Reel"—tunes that would ring in my head all week.

WHEELS

Cars passed the school so infrequently that our teacher looked out each time one went by. Although we pupils couldn't see the road unless we happened to be standing, we often knew by its sound which vehicle was passing. The milk truck rattled by each morning before school began, the mailman was predictably on schedule at 10:00 A.M., and from time to time farmers went by en route to or from town. Any other traffic was unusual, and if it happened to be a game warden's car, a cattle truck, or a motorcycle, we were allowed to stand up and look out, too.

Although nearly every rural family owned a motor car, most farmers seldom drove theirs more than once a week. A car was considered a luxury, since speed was not important, and anything people could conveniently do on foot or with a horse, they still did.

When I started school, a high percentage of the vehicles we saw were Model T Fords, and some of them had been around for many years. Yet it appeared that only a few men over age thirty had mastered the art of driving. Most farmers still felt more comfortable clutching a pair of reins than working a clutch. Prior to their getting a car, their previous experience with machinery had been limited to only three items that needed oil or grease: a milk-cream separator turned by hand, a team-drawn mowing machine used for cutting hay, and a dump rake that was pulled by a single horse. A few extremely avant-garde farmers owned noisy gasoline engines that operated a milking machine, a drag sawing machine, or a circular saw, and one enterprising man even had a threshing machine. But most were suspicious of any unfamiliar machinery and so terrified of the explosive power of gasoline that they handled their cars very timidly.

A great many older men drove as if they were still handling horses. We heard about one who had driven his car through the back of his barn yelling "Whoa" at the top of his lungs. Most everyone drove in the middle of the road, but some zig-zagged crazily from one ditch to another as they tried to keep track of what their neighbors were doing. They glanced at the road occasionally and until they began to feel they were in the ditch forgot completely that the car, unlike the horse, didn't know its way home.

My Uncle Henry, who learned to drive late in life, sometimes took me with him. Ordinarily he kept a slow, constant speed—about twenty miles per hour—on the narrow, winding roads, ensuring that no one could pass him. On corners, however, he tended to speed up and always assumed that no car was coming from the opposite direction. He didn't care for driving in villages, so he drove considerably faster through populated areas, causing pets and pedestrians to scurry, and even teenagers stared at him with amazement. Horns tooting and dirty looks bothered him not a bit, and if he noticed them at all, he always assumed they were meant for some careless driver. Although he drove for years without having an accident, he must have caused them frequently and frightened countless other drivers and passengers nearly to death.

Gears were mysterious to most old-timers, and a few made their entire trip in whichever gear the car was in when they started. Collisions were frequent, and there were as many caused by backing up as by going ahead. Some drivers looked as terrified to be on the road as we were to meet them there. Although "going like sixty" was an oft-used expression, the bumpy condition of our dirt roads and the horsepower of the cars made speeds of more than thirty-five extremely dangerous, and thus, unusual.

Roads were rough and thin tires never replaced until

absolutely necessary, so flats were the rule rather than the exception. Everyone expected at least one on any trip taken out of town. Repairing a tire was considered part of the price to be paid for the luxury of operating a car, and there was surprisingly little grumbling about it. Even covering the short distance to school, I sometimes came upon someone patching a tire.

Soon after I started school, one of my married brothers took me with his family on a trip to Willoughby Lake, a journey of about eighteen miles, one way. He had recently acquired a second-hand jet-black Model T and was very proud of it.

We were getting along just fine until, about three miles from home, a loud bang alerted us to our first flat tire. We all got out and stood around as my brother jacked up the car, removed the wheel, took off the tire, removed the tube, and repaired it with red rubber patches and smelly cement. Then he stuffed the tube back into the tire, mounted it on the wheel, put the wheel on the car, pumped up the tire, and let down the jack. As we hopped back to our places, he cranked up the car, and we were on our way once again. Two miles farther along, we heard another bang. The procedure was the same as before, but my brother's sputtering increased.

We had seven flat tires on that memorable thirty-six-mile trip, and while going down one long hill we looked out to see one of our front wheels rolling along beside us. It passed us and continued down the hill as the car lurched suddenly and stopped. It took some time to locate the wheel, find enough parts to hitch it back on, and to make the other necessary repairs.

Once we had to turn the car around on a steep hill and go up backward "so the gas could flow into the carburetor," my brother said. We made it to the top, all right, and without jumping up and down on the running board as he'd warned might be necessary. I never figured out how jumping would help, but it apparently was a common practice on steep hills.

The trip, including eating our picnic lunch, took all day.

I had never been on a long trip before, so it was a great adventure and I had a wonderful time. But, of course, I didn't have to crank the car and patch the tires.

Most of the women understood less about machinery than the men and thus were even more apprehensive of the motorized monsters. Very few attempted to drive them. Mrs. Kennison always rode in the back seat of their gray Model A Ford with her hand firmly placed on the handle of the door, which she kept slightly open. Her husband, sitting alone in the middle of the front seat with his large, callused hands gripping the steering wheel and his yellowed teeth clenching a pipe, looked like Ben Hur coming into the final turn.

My mother (and many other women new to the machine age) never felt entirely comfortable about any of us leaving home in a car, and she never relaxed until she was sure we were back. She absolutely refused to go for a drive until the house was neat from end to end. "If I get killed, I don't want someone else to have to clean up the place for a funeral," she said repeatedly.

She also made each of her children bathe and change clothes before any trip, even a short one to the store. We should, she said, always look and smell presentable to the public and not be a disgrace to the family. We all knew, however, that Ma's real concern was that we not have to be scrubbed up the first thing when they took us to the hospital or the undertaker's.

The young men took to the automotive age with more enthusiasm than their elders, and they treated their cars with far more loving care. They washed them often, and took them apart very professionally. The Jillson brothers had a few parts left over each time they reassembled their Maxwell, but they claimed, "As far as we can see, it runs better without them." Every young Henry Ford pretended he knew exactly how to adjust the spark, but none of them really understood what was happening. They all talked a great deal about double clutching and gasoline additives, and they argued endlessly with other car owners over which "make" was the best.

Torry Waugh's older brother, Perley, had a roadster, and with the top down, it made a dashing sight. All the girls were after him, and the schoolboys pleaded with him for a ride in his rumble seat, which he called a mother-in-law compartment. The more daring of us sometimes hitched short rides by standing on running boards and holding onto the window frame—a sport always frowned upon by our parents but that made us feel like the flashy sports we saw in the "Gasoline Alley" comic strip.

Bill Trout bought a musical horn for his car. It played "How Dry I Am," but Elwin Jillson said the notes actually relayed, "Not Paid for Yet." There was a lot of cocky talk about whose car could best outrun the highway patrol on their Harley-Davidson motorcycles, and there were frequent minor accidents as the younger drivers challenged one another to prove their boasts. Often on warm summer nights we heard the "cowboys" miles away, roaring down the road with cut-out mufflers and their horns blaring continuously. They burned up gas and tires, made a lot of smoke, and created much gossip as the older members of the community speculated about what else they were doing.

The only truck we saw regularly was driven by the man who started out at about four o'clock every morning to pick up the milk. Milk was taken to the creamery in ten-gallon metal cans with loose steel handles, and as the truck rattled along the bumpy roads, the noise could be heard for miles. Trucks had no radios, so the driver, possibly in an attempt to drown out the racket he was making, sang loudly.

Although the children in our neighborhood walked to school, many of our rural contemporaries who attended the big school in the village rode in the school team, a predecessor of the school bus. A pair of horses drew what looked like a big enclosed box with two tiny windows. It was placed on a sled during the winter and on wheels during mud season. In fall and late spring, however, the horse team was replaced by a motorized van. Several of these little buses shuttled the farm children into town from the outlying areas, and often the children of one family alone nearly filled the box. I seldom saw any of these conveyances, and I never envied anyone who had to ride to school in a wooden box.

Some motorists developed a car-driver relationship that was similar to the one they had previously held with their horses and buggies. They filled the interiors of their cars with dangling toys. A few stopped every dozen miles or so to let the car rest. Others patted their vehicles fondly or covered them with blankets on cold days. Both young and old drivers tended to take it out on their machines if they had any trouble. One man broke his leg while giving his car a swift kick after a minor mishap, and we heard that old Shep Irish took a horsewhip to his car one day when it refused to start. Worse yet was the man over in Sheffield who used a shotgun on his balky auto. Although the horse-and-buggy era was passing, the memory died hard.

HUNTING

Autumn was hunting season in northern Vermont. Different weeks were set aside to hunt various kinds of game, although woodchuck, squirrel, bobcat, porcupine, and fox could be shot all year, and skunks, too, were fair game anytime, especially if they were menacing your chickens. The rabbit and partridge season started in early October, but by far our most important season was deer hunting. It always began in mid-November and lasted for ten consecutive days, not including Sundays. Only male deer with antlers could be taken. It was difficult to ignore that season even if you did not hunt, because nearly all the men and boys, and even a few women, either hunted or pretended they did.

Most families felt that their grade-school children were too young for such serious business, but occasionally Brad Markres or some other boy in the seventh or eighth grade took along a rifle as he walked to school. The rest of us studied the Taylor or other mail-order catalogues and coveted all the hunting and trapping merchandise on display.

Since we weren't allowed to hunt, we spent a lot of time thinking up pranks. Sometimes, if there was a shot nearby at recess, one of the boys would yell "Did you get him, Mike?" Another would answer, "Yes, but he hain't got no horns." The dialogue was intended to excite all the other hunters—and possibly the game warden, if he happened to be in the neighborhood.

One November, Roger Lincoln's father was one of the rare lucky hunters. Roger brought a leg from the buck to school, and we spent part of the noon hour using it to make tracks in the snow and mud around a hunter's car that was parked nearby. We felt bad all afternoon that we wouldn't be able to stick around until he came out of the woods at dusk to find he had trudged many fruitless miles far back in the woods to no avail, while a deer had frolicked all around his parking place.

The first day of deer hunting was an unofficial state holiday, and most businesses in town closed so that their employees could hunt. During the 1930s, the local hunting was good, but the finding was poor. There were few deer because our farms were intensively grazed by cattle, leaving little brush for the wild animals to browse. For this reason most farm folks didn't take hunting too seriously and looked on the time as an excuse for a short vacation. Few were good shots, however, because the price of ammunition was high, and they had little free time for target practice. To most of our neighbors, "going hunting" meant taking a rusty old .30/.30 Winchester or a 12-gauge shotgun out of the closet, putting a few shells and a jackknife in their pockets, and heading for the woods after morning chores. They might or might not tie a red bandana around their hat as a warning to other hunters.

All the mothers felt that their children should wear some red when walking to school, so our usual drab caps and jackets were decorated with pieces of red and orange cloth throughout the season. I never felt in any danger because I knew that bullets cost three cents each and were far too expensive to waste on anything less valuable than a deer. Little Torry Waugh was more cautious than most of us, however. He had been so scared by his parents' warnings that he felt his red hat was a kind of protective helmet, and he never dared take it off until he was safely inside the building. He wouldn't blow his nose outside, either, fearing that some poor-sighted hunter would mistake his handkerchief for the white tail of a deer.

To us schoolboys, the hunting season was far more exciting than the upcoming Thanksgiving holiday. When we were coloring pilgrims, turkeys, and Indians to decorate the school windows, we talked endlessly about the different calibers and advantages of all the guns we would own one day. We collected all the empty rifle cartridges and shotgun shells we could find, and at recess we swapped the different sizes.

Although hunting was not considered a reliable way for a man to feed his family, it was an acceptable excuse for him to get off the farm and stop working for a few hours without being considered a lazy lout. Simply going for a walk in the woods was unheard of in any season. A man could, if he were "huntin'," however, legitimately socialize with other hunters, brag a bit over hunting experiences, and perhaps explore some new territory. Like winning a raffle at Grange, there was always a slim chance that he might get a deer or at least see a fresh track. Snort Finney said he had put his .38/.55 cartridges in and out of his old rifle every season for twenty-seven years and had never shot it once. He mused, "Them shells are so worn out now, I doubt they'd even fire." Jed Prior confessed that he had carried an unloaded gun for years and got as much game as 99 percent of all the hunters he met.

Because these were the hunters I'd grown up with, I got a real start when I saw my first "city" hunter from "away." One morning on my way to school, I saw a car parked near one of our fields, with several men standing around it. They were taking shiny rifles out of beautiful new brown leather cases. In their brilliant fire-red woolen coats, caps, and breeches, they looked quite different from the overalled farmers who went directly from barn to woods in the same clothes.

Full of curiosity, I stopped to talk with them and to look them over at closer range so that I could describe them properly to the other kids at school. Hatchets, revolvers, long hunting knives, compasses, and coils of rope hung from their wide leather belts. Field glasses were draped around their necks, and one man was studying a map.

They asked me where to find the best hunting, and I helpfully told them that most people went into the Black Hill area by way of Skunk Hollow, three miles away, and pointed in that direction. They muttered something about country kids not being hunters, and with no thanks or farewell, they started off in the direction of our maple woods, where not even a deer track had been seen for twenty years. I continued on my way to school, hurt that they had ignored my advice. I was also resentful that they had a map of our woods and were acting as if it were their own.

Although the deer season lasted less than two weeks, most local men felt guilty about wasting time and so went back to work after a few days. The city hunters, more persistent, hung around for the entire season. Some even got deer, much to the disgust of the farmers, who felt that the herd belonged to them since they had fed them all year.

The few lucky local hunters proudly took their trophies to the reporting station, then hung them in a tree or open shed a few days for their neighbors to covet. The great majority came home empty-handed but they always managed to collect a lot of stories to tell in future years.

Because Thanksgiving Day was considered a holiday, it was traditional to go hunting that morning. Even the men who seldom hunted felt that they should take to the woods while their womenfolk were fixing dinner. Once one of my brothers, while following a track on a dark, snowy day, got lost in the deep woods and finally had to follow his own tracks back. Meanwhile my mother fretted and worried about who had shot whom as she tried to keep the dinner warm. Although dinner was sometimes delayed for the hunters, it was always worth waiting for, even if the promised venison was not part of the delicacies.

We never had turkey or cranberries, but the long table in our dining room was always covered with two or three fat chickens, a roast of pork, mountains of vegetables, and pumpkin and mince pie. Everything was home grown except the coffee, raisins, and some grapes and walnuts my married brothers and their families had brought.

In spite of the anticipation with which we all looked forward to hunting, everyone breathed a deep sigh of relief when the season was over, the flatlanders went back where they belonged, and we could all think about Christmas.

POLITICS, PROSPERITY, AND GOOD SPIRITS

"Democrat" was a nasty word, at home or at school. We seldom used it but saved it as an expletive for special occasions when no ordinary cuss word seemed adequate. When we played teams, often the North was pitted against the South, Cowboys versus Indians, or Colonists against Redcoats. When anyone suggested playing Republicans versus Democrats, however, there was always a ruckus. No one would volunteer to be on the side of the New Dealers.

I hadn't ever seen one and wasn't at all sure that I wanted to. The grown-ups began to use the word often, about the time I first started school, and always in a disgusting tone. Herbert Hoover was president, and apparently Franklin D. Roosevelt and a man named John Nance Garner were giving him a lot of grief. Democrats were still practically unheard of in our parts, even though Waldo Markres thought he might have seen one run through the woods, but he hadn't had his gun with him at the time. Lath Rice had heard that there was a stuffed one in the museum in St. Johnsbury, though he confessed that he'd never seen it.

Naturally, all of us were stunned when we learned that two Democrats had voted in our township in the election of 1932. Two Democrats actually lived among us! It was five years later and I was out of elementary school before I first met a Democrat in person. I remember being very surprised to find that he seemed proud of his affiliation. I had expected a Democrat to be rather apologetic and chagrined, somewhat the way you feel when someone discovers you are wearing two different-colored socks.

No Vermonter worth his johnny-cake and maple syrup ever considered Calvin Coolidge anything less than a great president. Neither he nor Hoover caught any blame in our neighborhood for the hard times we were experiencing. The Depression, we were sure, had been caused by the Wall Street bankers, railroad barons, labor unions, the Fitzgeralds, the Roosevelts, and, of course, the Al Smith gang, with probably a little help from the pope, the liquor makers, and the *Literary Digest*.

"Republican," we were made to understand early in life, "is synonymous with virtue, hard work, honesty, thrift, and behaving one's self," whereas "Democrat" meant "waste, laziness, welfare, drunken revelry, crime, and probably godlessness." Furthermore, there were three kinds of Democrats: the out-and-out rascals, the feather-brained intellectuals, and the millions of not-too-bright ordinary citizens whom Mr. Roosevelt, their leader, consistently managed to fool by making them think he was on their side.

Our scorn of Roosevelt and his cronies reached a peak in the second term of the New Deal when large numbers of WPA, CCC, and other "alphabet soup" gangs descended to survey land and catalogue the cemetery stones in our area. We were completely unprepared for this invasion and stared in amazement as CCC youths in baggy khaki pants marched past our school single file, like the seven dwarfs in the Snow White story. We soon learned that they were clearing out old roads in the woods near the school, and one day we noticed that a tall fire tower had appeared on Burke Mountain twenty miles away.

Once, as the strangers passed the school, someone pointed out the first black man any of us had ever seen. We talked about him for days. We laughed to see young men sporting beards, and we heard Spanish and Italian spoken for the first time. Listening to these newcomers, we picked up a few colorful city-type obscenities that sounded just great but that had to be used very cautiously.

Another cloudy fall morning two surveyors were working around the schoolhouse with a transit, a pole, and some large charts. Our teacher, Mrs. Marshall, thinking it a good opportunity to broaden our outlook, invited them in to tell us what they were doing.

Although they seemed like grown-up, sophisticated city men to us, they were probably only in their early twenties. They explained the topical mapping they were doing and how a transit worked, and they answered our many questions. Finally the teacher caught on to the fact that we were inventing queries merely so the visitors would stay longer and delay classes. She thanked them and bade them goodbye.

Roger Lincoln shot out one final question: "Where are you going to work this afternoon?"

"North of here," one of them answered, "but we're hoping it will rain so we won't have to work at all. We get paid just the same."

After they had gone, Mrs. Marshall, who was well past fifty and one of the few teachers we had who weren't just out of school, began to rave. "The very idea, wanting it to rain so one won't have to work—and to get paid for pure idleness," she said in disgust. During the day she repeated the same theme in different ways, making sure that each of us thoroughly understood the evils that lurked in the ways of the flatland intruders. None of them was ever invited in again.

Our hard-working Yankee parents made no attempt to conceal their contempt for the outlanders' work habits either, and we were not encouraged to talk to them. It was often repeated that four WPA loafers were needed to do the work of one honest man. One of our neighbors said that if they were mowing a lawn there would be one coming, one going, one resting, and one mowing. The initial letters of Works Progress Administration was quickly interpreted to mean "We Putter Around," and our elders worried considerably that the impressionable youth of the area would acquire the sinful notions and slothful habits of these urban immigrants.

The CCC and WPA boys, no doubt unaware of the sins attributed to them, were only the forerunners of the changing age. By the late 1930s the New Deal had moved into our lives, and long after it was too late, the Yankee farmers discovered that they, too, were entangled in the political system they hated so intensely. They were buying lime and fertilizer at below-market prices, collecting parity and subsidy checks and letting the government set the price of their milk. Federal experts were now telling them how to manage their farms. The proud farmers, once as independent as the west wind, now stood meekly by as well-dressed milk inspectors from Boston ordered them to clean up their stables, keep the manure spread, and put in refrigeration—or else the neat little license to produce and sell milk that was tacked to each milkroom wall would be taken away.

The result was even more resentment against any type of "progress" and made the farmers even more eager to vote against anything that suggested less freedom. We knew lots of people like the old Vermonter who, at age eighty-five, was interviewed by a city newspaper.

"You've seen every change that took place during the twentieth century," the reporter said, "and there have been a lot of them."

"A-ya," said the old gentleman after long thought, "and I've been agin' every one of em."

When Roosevelt was campaigning in 1932, the repeal of Prohibition had been one of his foremost promises. One day I'd been allowed to ride to the village with Uncle Henry. A car parked in front of the store bore the message: "Bring Back Beer. More Work, More Money, More Prosperity."

I puzzled over it, reading it carefully. "Do you think bringing back beer will mean more work?" I asked my ultra-conservative uncle, who was viewing the slogan with considerable scorn. "More work for the sheriff," he snorted.

Prohibition had not affected most folks in our small, law-abiding neighborhood, since there had been little tippling previously. There were two theories regarding the prim and proper old Yankees and Demon Rum. One was that they were too righteous and moral to drink, and the other, that they were merely too "gol' 'ram" stingy to buy the stuff but would eagerly lap it up if it were given to them.

There were minor exceptions to the local general abstinence. We all knew that Harry McCuen made home brew out of grain and malt in the west corner of town; and Ozzie Munn, who distilled cedar oil for his livelihood, was reputed to run a batch of "corn likker" through his apparatus now and then. Two or three old residents still combed the woods, gathering wild sarsaparilla and other roots for fermented root beer, and some enterprising sugar makers made the last run of the maple trees each season into sap beer. A few French-Canadian farmers made wine from carrots, rhubarb, chokecherries, and dandelion blossoms. That was the extent of the neighborhood moonshining.

Some liquor was imported, however, mostly for the summer residents who could afford it. Ted Lyford, who lived in an adjoining mountain town, peddled meat around the lake twice a week all summer. Not only did he butcher large numbers of animals and deliver ice, but he also had a friend who ran liquor from Canada, brewed beer, and made hard cider. His meat wagon held a hidden compartment concealed by the steaks and sausage, and he was an important part of the community for several years. Most people bought only meat from him, however, and never could understand how he paid for his farm so fast.

In neighboring towns Prohibition had a decided effect, and its repeal in 1933, in spite of my uncle's prediction, probably gave the sheriff less work. Repeal brought an end to the smuggling across the border from Canada, thirty miles away. The smuggling had made an exciting and profitable business for some enterprising citizens and resulted in some hair-raising stories.

Most of the time the rum runners avoided our narrow crooked roads, but we heard of exciting chases down the valley highway that ran north and south through our town. One evening Max Donnigan, who lived near the turn to our hill, was closing his big barn doors when a huge Packard tore around the corner and drove up his high drive into the barn. While an open-mouthed Max stood by, the man ordered him to shut the doors "quick." Just after he did, a border patrol car zoomed by, rounded the corner, and roared out of sight. What happened between Max and the smuggler we never knew, but very likely some Canadian whiskey or American money stayed in town that night.

"By gol'," Max told us later. "That car was so dang loaded, it broke right through the floor, where me and my horses hauled big loads of hay all summer."

Sometimes, quite late on a warm summer evening, I listened fascinated from my upstairs bedroom window as John Barker's hired men walked home after a dance or the fair, singing "Show Me the Way to Go Home" or "I'm an Old Cow Hand from the Rio Grande" at the top of their throaty voices. The serenades went on, chorus after chorus, until they finally staggered over the rise and out of earshot. In spite of lots of talk, and all the bragging about how much 3.2 beer one could drink, usually there was more noise than trouble, and the sheriff never got very busy in our neighborhood during the '30s.

Despite all our fears, too, the two Democrats in town actually turned out to be pillars of the Congregational Church and were tee-totaling, respectable citizens in every way. On the other hand, directly after repeal, several of the solid old Republicans were seen sneaking into Bruno's Tavern over in the next town.

Contrary to what Franklin D. had promised us, the repeal of Prohibition didn't end the Depression, but it did give us something different to think about for several months.

CHRISTMAS

In early December we peeled the cut-out turkeys, Pilgrims, and Indians off the school windows and began to replace them with bells, stars, and Christmas trees. Since a foot of snow usually covered the ground, we already felt we were in the midst of the holiday season. During our morning exercises, we sang Christmas carols instead of "Swanee River" and "America the Beautiful," and Teacher passed out the recitations and parts for plays we were to learn for our Christmas program.

Our excitement mounted as the great day approached. The older kids spoke of previous school Christmas parties and the cookies, fudge, and cupcakes their mothers had brought in. We drew names for the one person to whom we were to give a gift, but we always swapped the slips around to get a name we really wanted.

Since none of us ever had a chance to visit a store during the Christmas season, we spent many hours looking over the Sears Roebuck and Montgomery Ward mail-order catalogues, and in our imaginations we made out long lists of the things we dreamed some fabulously rich, unknown benefactor would give us. I cut from magazines, as did everyone else, the pictures of coveted bicycles, erector sets, sports equipment, clothes, games, and weapons. We always took sheets of cut-outs to school to share our dreams with our friends, knowing there was absolutely no chance of getting even one of the things we longed for.

Roger and Bradley Lincoln brought from home catalogues that especially whetted our appetites. The fat Taylor catalogue listed hundreds of traps, guns, baits, and other hunting and trapping paraphernalia; and Johnson Smith's, although smaller in size, was even thicker and filled with hundreds of pages of fascinating merchandise. All the mail-order catalogues were called "wish books," with good reason.

During the first three weeks in December, we spent a half hour each day practicing for our Christmas program. As the Friday before Christmas drew near, our teachers usually became more and more desperate and realized that we would need at least two hours of practice each day in order to produce a passable show. So each day we said our "pieces," sang songs, and performed the little plays over and over.

The annual ritual of getting the tree was nearly as important as the program. Each year when I was very young, I looked longingly after the lucky boys who had been chosen for that great adventure. By the time I was eleven, it was finally my turn. Three days before the program, after our morning exercises, Miss Reynolds sent four of us into the woods, warning us several times that we should be back in less than an hour—even though Robert Coomer explained to her that it usually took much longer than that to find a really good tree. As I trailed the three older boys into the woods, we passed many trees that looked perfectly fine to me, but the more experienced of our crew didn't think so. We walked about five miles, examining hundreds of balsam firs, red and white spruce, and even a few pine and cedar trees, wondering what Miss Reynolds would say if we brought in one of those. As usual, no one asked the farmer who owned the land if we could cut down one of his trees, but we knew he wouldn't mind, since it was for the school.

Finally, when it was nearly noon, we trudged back toward school and with our axe cut down one of the first trees we had looked at. This, I learned later, was how it had always been done. It took the four of us pulling together to drag the heavy spruce up the hill to the schoolhouse, but we were excited and very proud of our choice.

The teacher was well braced for the usual tree expedition excuses for our tardiness. "Couldn't find a good one." "The axe was powerful dull." (That one was true.) "Uphill all the way." She knew as well as we that the morning arithmetic class was the real reason for the delay.

During the lunch hour, as the snow covering the tree melted over the schoolhouse floor, we sawed off the butt and nailed on boards in an *X* shape for our tree stand. As usual, we had chosen a thick, prickly white spruce, known locally as a cat spruce. Or, if it had grown in an open pasture, as ours had, it was called a bull spruce. Although white spruce are beautiful trees, as soon as they are put in a warm room they emit a strong, strange odor that accounts for still another local name of theirs—skunk spruce. It was reminiscent of the Christmas season and didn't smell bad to us, since most of us had white spruce trees in our living rooms at home, but I heard one girl remark that she wished just once we would bring back a nice fragrant balsam fir tree, even if it were not so bushy.

In addition to our usual lessons and daily practice for our program, each year we made decorations for the tree. This was considered recreation rather than art, and it was done mostly at recess. From home we brought colored paper, ribbon, and pieces of foil that had been wrapped around compressed yeast cakes. Under the teacher's guidance we shaped these materials into simple chains, circles, and stars. One year we popped corn on a kerosene stove the teacher had brought to school and strung it together with some wild highbush cranberries Charlie Forge had found in a hedgerow.

The first year I helped to cut the tree, our trimmings were very special because Miss Reynolds brought some store-bought decorations from her home. Shiny tinsel, silver icicles, red roping, streamers, and sparkling little glass balls were all things we had never seen before. But most thrilling and unusual of all was a string of colored lights that she attached to an automobile battery lent her by the farmer with whom she boarded. When she turned on the switch the day of the program, we were breathless. We couldn't take our eyes off the most beautiful sight any of us had ever seen. No Christmas tree in the past or future would ever surpass that one.

The program always took place on the Friday before Christmas, and because the days are so short in December, it started promptly at one o'clock. Unlike the Halloween festivities, the fathers and older boys almost never attended the Christmas party, and to many, even Christmas Day was simply one more workday. But the mothers and other women of the neighborhood came, and they brought along their little children. As at Halloween, we had to bring a few planks inside from the woodshed to make room for everybody. Most women came on foot, and some pulled their babies on sleds. Occasionally a man brought his womenfolk in a sleigh and returned for them after the festivities were over.

The older boys and girls had a great advantage over the little ones when it came to performing in a school program. Even those who had not spent two years in each grade had heard the songs and pieces so many times that they were familiar. My first year in school, however, the Christmas program was another baffling event for which I was completely unprepared. I was barely six years old and had never seen a movie or, except at our Halloween program, heard pieces spoken.

Gradually I realized that the play I was part of was a "let's pretend" situation, since it was about a family spending Christmas with their grandmother. My part was small. I had to open a package, take out a jacket, and act very delighted with my "gift." When someone nudged me, I dutifully said, "Oh, Grandma, thank you" and managed to go in the right direction when someone else shoved me, but I had no notion of what was happening.

Over the years, although the quality of my acting improved very little, I became more knowledgeable about school programs and Christmas. Every teacher tried, without much success, to get us to act more professional, but we were all country folk. David Finney swayed from side to side while speaking a piece, and I always tried to stand nervously on one leg, "like a little banty rooster," according to one teacher. Myra Temple consistently began to speak as soon as her piece was announced. By the time she arrived at the front of the room, her recitation was well underway, and she was quite breathless. She also headed for her seat before she was finished and spoke the final few words just as she was sitting down.

The year I was in the eighth grade we had an optimistic teacher who saw no reason why her eight charges, ages six to fifteen, couldn't produce Dickens's A *Christmas Carol*. Naturally she abridged the story a great deal, and most of the older children had to play several parts. Each day Steve Markres, who was playing the part of the three different ghosts, forgot to bring the chain he had promised to school. Under threat of punishment from the teacher, however, he remembered on the day of the performance. In the midst of the production, he dragged in a heavy, twenty-foot logging chain that weighed nearly seventy-five pounds. The poor teacher nearly had what was then called a conniption fit, and I, a nightshirted Scrooge, dropped my candle. The delighted audience enjoyed the comic relief since they were all unfamiliar with the story and were rather bewildered about what we were trying to do.

After the last song was finished, Santa Claus arrived amidst jingling bells. His coat and boots smelled heavily of the barn, but real frost hung on his whiskers. He distributed our gifts from the teacher, the ones we had given her, and those we were exchanging with one another. Most of the boys received small metal cars or airplanes marked "Made in Japan," card games such as Authors, books, or small pouches holding three or four pencils. The girls' gifts were usually face powder, tiny bottles of cologne, or books about nurses. The teacher invariably received box after box of gift handkerchiefs.

The small babies were passed around and admired, and we all devoured the homemade candy, popcorn balls, cookies, and maple fudge our mothers had brought. Roger Lincoln and Charlie Forge, after they'd opened their presents and eaten, were ready to start a game outdoors, but the rest of us opted to stay by the big wood furnace and eat more.

The smell of cat spruce, popcorn, and wood smoke hung in the air, mingling with a powerful fragrance of mothballs from Mrs. Waugh's winter coat, not long out of summer storage. As usual, Mrs. Wright's teeth, which she wore only on special occasions, kept dropping down as she chatted, a phenomenon that fascinated us all, but especially little Laurie Finney, who stood for some time staring open-mouthed at her.

Everyone wore so many clothes that it took a long time for the crowd to leave, but finally coats, hats, and leggings—those long, heavy, footless stockings we all wore—were sorted out and the children buttoned up. The last little runny nose was given a final wipe, and under parental prompting everyone said their "Much obligeds" and "Thank yous" as the crowd tromped out into the cold, snowy afternoon.

A few older boys and girls lingered to help Miss Reynolds clean up the schoolroom. We removed the trimmings from our beautiful spruce tree, gently tipped it over, and took it outside into the early winter darkness. Then, with shouts of "See you next year," we started home in different directions, each clutching a game or book, exhilarated by the events of the afternoon and an awareness that school was over for a couple of weeks.

I knew that another Christmas celebration would soon be upcoming at home. For the next week the house would smell deliciously of freshly baked pies and bread every time I came in from the barn, and Aunt Agnes would be coming soon to visit us, making her famous home-dipped chocolates and divinity. I would be put to work, as I was each year, cracking bushels of butternuts for maple-butternut fudge.

I had no money to spend at Christmas, so I made gifts in secret. Each year, like most of the other boys I knew, I produced a collection of bookends, bird houses, potholder hangers, and doorstops from scraps of lumber. I wrapped them in wrinkled colored paper salvaged from the school party and previous Christmas celebrations and carefully hid them in the attic until Christmas afternoon, when we'd have our tree.

The year I was twelve, on Christmas Eve we went to the service and tree celebration at the church in the village. In spite of a crystal-clear sky full of sparkling stars and a brilliant display of northern lights, the long ride in the open sleigh was so chilly it was far from pleasant. We were bundled up in sheepskin coats and wool touques, scarves, leggings, and two sets of mittens, and we were covered with a buffalo lap robe that was a half century old. Still I shivered with the cold as I peered out at the sparkling snow. I wondered if a bright star in the western sky was the Christmas star.

When we arrived at the church, one of my brothers unhitched Molly from the sleigh as I clutched the lantern. He covered her with a blanket and led her into the church horsebarn, which was only slightly warmer than outdoors. We tied her in an empty stall next to dozens of other steaming horses, blew out the lantern, and went toward the church.

As we walked through the door into the sanctuary, I quickly forgot my cold nose and frozen feet. Soft carols were being played on the big church organ, the room was lighted by flickering candles, and a huge evergreen tree covered with candy boxes and gifts stood in the front corner.

Although the church was very cold and many women and men kept on their coats, I barely noticed the heavy mothball aroma as I quickly became absorbed in the Youth Group's pageant and pieces. The older children in the village had more poise and confidence than we at our school, and their singing was far better than ours, but I was grateful to see that the youngest children acted as confused as I had at my early performances. One pre-schooler, after finishing his piece, called out, "How did you like that, Mommy and Daddy? Pretty good, huh?" The resulting laughter seemed to make the chilly sanctuary warmer.

Finally we had the tree. Santa came, better dressed and more realistic appearing than the one we had at school. I felt a bit left out because I was not part of the Sunday school classes that received gifts, but he handed a bag of popcorn and candy to each child. I enjoyed that, even though I was a manly twelve years old. As we once again bundled up and walked into the crisp starry night to hitch up Molly, I vowed never to miss another Christmas Eve service, even if I had to walk in a blizzard.

Christmas morning was so cold that a heavy frost covered all the windows, but for once it wasn't difficult to get out of bed. Until I was eight years old I had hung my stocking in back of the Round Oak stove. Although twelve was far too old for that, I still missed doing it a little bit and remembered the chocolate bar, orange, and tiny toy that used to be waiting when I came downstairs.

We did the chores early on Christmas morning, because there was so much to do with more than twenty of our family coming home. The cows, horses, and hens always got extra feed, not only because we thought they should celebrate, too, but also because we expected to be late in feeding them that night.

Snow always seemed to fall on Christmas Day, creating Christmas-card scenery but making travel difficult. Some of my aunts and uncles and older brothers with their families drove their cars as far as the roads were plowed, then walked the rest of the way. Others came by horse and sleigh. I had to shovel the paths extra wide and help cover up the sleighs with robes and blankets as they arrived.

The smell of roasting chicken, pork, and freshly baked rolls made it seem to me as if the last relative would never arrive so we could eat. Finally, when everyone had gathered and the dinner was ready, my little nieces and nephews were seated on mail-order catalogues so that they could reach their food. Five extra leaves had been put in the heavy oak table, and I wondered if the massive legs would be able to support all that food. It seemed to me that Uncle Fred's blessing was far too long, but at last the food was passed around. Besides our usual fare, we had some exotic treats that had been brought in by our relatives, including grapes, sweet potatoes, and a new, exciting, bright-red, wiggly food called Jell-O. Everything looked, smelled, and tasted so delicious that I nearly forgot to save space for Aunt Agnes's blueberry pie, the wonderful maple butternut fudge we'd made, and the walnuts, ribbon candy, peach blossoms, and peanut brittle the relatives had brought.

It seemed as if many interminable hours passed before the dishes were finally washed and put away so we could take the presents off the tree. Uncle Bert, especially, was in no hurry and kept reminiscing about holidays when he was a lad. He had no trouble waiting for his gifts, since he knew he'd get a half dozen pairs of dress-up socks, as usual, and he already had more than he could possibly wear, since he seldom dressed up. My little nephews, nieces, and I were more impatient. All day we had been sneaking glances at the piles of gifts under the tree and had found several interesting packages with our names on them. To our dismay, even after we had all sat down we were made to wait even longer because Aunt Marion felt the assembled gathering should have some "pieces." My nieces, nephews, and I each had to recite a poem we'd learned for school Christmas programs. Sometimes she tried to make us sing a carol, too, but we were spared that this particular year.

Finally the grown-ups were ready, and they selected three of the youngest children who could read to pass out the gifts. The still younger ones helped them, at least until they got a gift themselves and stopped to open it. I knew that the skis, radio, camera, rifle, and typewriter I'd dreamed about would not be there. Instead, I got some heavy wool mittens Ma had stayed up all night to make, some warm winter pants, a game of Anagrams, and a brown-and-white touque, a Fameuse apple, a Tom Swift book, some pencils, and a notebook. I watched carefully as my family opened the bookends, doorstops, and pasted-up scrap books I'd so carefully wrapped for them. They seemed to be delighted and made no comment about the lopsided carpentry.

Sally, a niece who was nearly my age, gave me a peanut wrapped in layer after layer of paper. The others laughed as I unwrapped the big package. It was fun, and in those Depression times we all knew we were very lucky. Probably there were people in our own town who didn't have a real Christmas dinner.

Dusk fell soon after 3:30, and our visitors always wanted to get off our hill before dark, especially if snow was falling or it looked like a storm. Uncle Burt, who was not accustomed to country roads, got his sleigh stuck and sputtered a lot as we dug and pushed him out. We watched until he was over the hill and out of sight, knowing he wouldn't venture over our road again until the mud was dried out, in late May.

When the last company had left, we changed into our old pants, overalls, and boots and did the chores by the light of our flickering, smoky lanterns. The barn seemed more warm and peaceful than usual, as if the cows and horses, too, realized that it was a special time.

None of us was very hungry, even after we had finished the chores and returned to the house, but we nibbled at all the wonderful leftovers anyway. Before I went to bed I had time to look at my new book, and we played the new game of Flinch my sister had received. As I slid into the cold bed in my warm flannel pajamas, the heated freestones at the foot felt good. My tummy rolled a bit from too many unfamiliar sweets. Every few minutes our old house snapped loudly with the frost, a reminder that winter was here to stay. But under the warm cozy quilts it was still Christmas, and I felt good thinking about it.

MIDWINTER DAY

After the Christmas holidays we settled into winter. New Year's Day, except for putting a new almanac near the telephone and hanging new calendars, was barely noticed. Like everyone else, we got calendars from the bank, from Dr. Miles' Laboratories someplace out west, from the Raleigh man, the garage, and several stores. We hung them all, sometimes several in each room. Most were decorated with pictures of bowls of flowers, little boys fishing, or comic paintings, such as the one of a city tourist being chased from a farm pasture by a snorting bull. The bank calendar had a photograph of its big brick building, and one storekeeper always proclaimed in big letters that he had been over a half century at the same stand.

Both the Dr. Miles calendar and the almanac confidently gave the weather for each day of the year, which we always enjoyed reading, especially since it often turned out just the opposite. No matter what was predicted, we knew most winter days would be snowy and cold.

Throughout my childhood I heard stories about Vermonters in earlier times who habitually froze up their old folks in the winter, buried them in a snowbank, and thawed them out in the spring. No one I asked knew anyone personally who had been given this treatment, but many people seemed to half believe it had been done and thought it was a good idea. Winter was very long in our mountains, and every fall Josh McLaren said he wished there was an easy way to pass up the season entirely and take a shortcut directly into May.

One of the worst ordeals of winter for me was getting out of a cozy bed on a cold, dark morning. Our old farmhouse had no heat in the bedrooms upstairs, except for a slight amount that came through the floor registers and quickly disappeared through the uninsulated ceilings, walls, and frosty window panes. On the coldest nights, my mother would heat several soapstones on the stove, wrap each one in a towel, and give us each one to put at the foot of the bed. Although the stone cooled long before morning, the bed stayed warm, thanks to many layers of quilts and blankets that held in the body heat.

Ma's "Time to get up!" made me conscious of my cold nose, and I dreaded touching the wood floor with my bare feet. Through sleepy eyes I could see that the half glass of water left on my bureau the night before was covered with thick ice, and I watched my breath come out in white puffs, as if from a fire-breathing dragon. Gradually I became aware that I was needed in the barn to help feed the cattle, so I'd grab my clothes and run downstairs to dress by the hot wood stove. David Finney claimed that his father accidentally let the fire go out one night, and in the morning he ran across the road in his underwear to dress in the warm barn.

I didn't object to doing chores in the winter, because our barn was surprisingly warm too, even on the coldest nights, thanks to the body heat of our small herd of Holsteins. Unfortunately, because we had no running water in the barn, the animals had to be let outdoors twice each day to drink from the concrete tub in the barnyard—after we'd chopped the ice from the top—and that cooled off the barn. We cleaned out the manure before we let the cows out to drink, because when the doors were left open for several minutes, not only the manure but also the water we carried for the calves and everything else would begin to freeze.

We always did the milking before breakfast, and the food on the table looked good as we tramped into the house. Ma believed firmly that the only proper way to start any day, winter or summer, was with a big bowl of hot oatmeal that would "stick to our ribs." She put it on the wood stove just before she went to bed, and it simmered all night in a double boiler. Every morning she made a batch of graham rolls, and occasionally we had fried potatoes left over from supper although, unlike some of our more traditional neighbors, we never had mince pie for breakfast. Sundays were always an exception to this daily fare, because instead of oatmeal, we had cornmeal cooked the same way. We never had cornmeal except on Sunday because Ma felt that there was no real energy in corn, and one could never do a day's work on it. "Corn is for fattening hogs," she declared. I always looked forward to Sundays and cornmeal "mush," not only because it was a welcome change from oatmeal but also because we always poured almost as much maple syrup over it as milk.

After breakfast on schooldays I changed out of barn clothes, bundled up in my heavy woolens, and, clutching my lunch pail, ran most of the way to school. I used to wonder if the cold-looking chickadees along the way were wishing they had followed the bobolinks south.

Most January days, even the warm oatmeal, clothes, and exercise didn't keep me from being nearly frozen by the time I arrived at school. We all backed up to the big wood heater, trying to thaw out, but I continued to shiver. With each arriving child, the open door let in blasts of Arctic air, and the large windows were soon covered with thick frost from our steamy breaths. The morning school chores helped us older boys get warm as we carried in mountains of firewood to keep the stove roaring, lugged the water from the Tyler farm, shoveled the path, and dug snow off the woodshed roof when it got too heavy. Although Steve Markres, who did the janitorial work, always had a good fire started when we arrived, every object in the room had become freezing cold overnight, and many days we continued to see our breath until mid-morning and didn't take off our jackets until nearly noon.

It was distressing to find that the world globe that hung near the ceiling was always toasty hot when we pulled it down, since all the warm air collected there. The cold air settled about our feet like bees around a saucer of honey. Furthermore, to keep the stove burning a large amount of warm air continually roared up the chimney. This was quickly replaced by sub-zero air that poured into the room like white fog through numerous cracks around the doors and windows.

On those days it didn't make us feel any better to hear Rose and Lily's warnings about what happened to people who got really cold: "If your feet freeze, they must be cut off immediately, with an axe if no doctor is handy, or a disease called gangrene will set in." "Frostbite on your face turns it all black, and your skin falls off in sheets." And every cold day, Rose continued to warn everyone about the danger of "chill-brains." "If your head gets too cold, all the gray matter inside will jell and become utterly useless," she maintained.

Somehow we all managed to retain our skin, limbs, and whatever gray matter we had, but during the coldest and most blizzardy January and February days, we played indoors during most recesses. The teacher saw no point in letting us all get dressed and undressed, which was quite a chore, for only a few minutes of outdoor play. Play time had been severely curtailed anyway, since because of the short days our noon hour had been cut in half so that we could start home before it got dark.

We didn't much mind staying indoors most days at that time of year. The little children liked to play musical games using a wind-up phonograph the teacher had brought in, and we heard "Farmer in the Dell" and "London Bridge" over and over. The older ones played Fruit Basket, Hangman, Hide the Thimble, Button Button, and similar games. We exchanged ideas and traded jokes we had read somewhere or heard from our older brothers and sisters. Knock-knock jokes were just beginning, and we loved them. "Who's there?" "Ohio lady." "Ohio lady who?" "I didn't know you could yodel." The "Little Audrey" stories were popular one year. She always laughed and laughed, and we did, too. Once she fell out of an airplane and laughed and laughed all the way down because she was wearing a light fall coat.

Even after Christmas we continued to study the Sears and Wards catalogues and pored over the ads in newspapers and *Farm Journal, Youth's Companion,* and *Country Home* that we brought to school to read and swap. We "ordered" thousands of dollars' worth of goods, dreaming of all the happiness money could buy. The boys' favorites were submachine guns offered for three or four hundred dollars, rifles, silencers, Bowie knives, crossbows, and other weapons. We coveted the self-help books that would show us how to be devastatingly popular with the opposite sex, how to build mighty muscles, and how to get rid of pimples. We were very curious about the salves that were said to cure any sore and to get rid of the warts that we all had, and we wondered about the electric belts that would banish lameness and restore lost manhood. We were especially intrigued by the books that laid bare all the hidden secrets of sex, the Orient, the Masons, and the Ku Klux Klan.

Had we been men of means, we'd have purchased gadgets that would let us throw our voices into trunks and corners (what fun we could have with the teacher!), and X-ray eyepieces that would let us count the bones in our hands. I would have ordered a leather jacket for $4.95, a .22 rifle for $4.00, or an air gun for half that. A .38 snubnose revolver that any Chicago mobster would have been proud to own could be ours for $6.98 plus postage. Nothing was ever said in the ads about the necessity of being over age twenty-one or needing to get one's parents' permission.

Some newspaper and magazine ads advertised bicycles, books, hatchets, scooters, and Boy Scout uniforms that could be ours absolutely free if we were to sell salve, magazines, cosmetic kits, or home medical guides to "our grateful neighbors and friends." Many magazines carried small but tempting ads promising big money if we would raise foxes, minks, chinchillas, capons, bees, or ginseng. We could get instant fame and fortune if we were to sign up for a course in taxidermy, buy a printing press, or learn how to repair the newfangled radios. For the price of a postage stamp we could get more details about how to write poetry and short stories for the many magazines that were clamoring for new talent, or we could compose country and western songs for the numerous singers desperately awaiting our genius and anxious to pay top dollar for them.

Since we didn't possess the three cents necessary to buy the stamp to learn more about those exciting opportunities, we went on being poor and uninformed. Anyway, we knew that even if we were to try to sell the magazines, salves, or greeting cards, there was no one in our neighborhood who had money for such foolishness. Each year the Thompson sub remained only a dream, luckily, as did the miner's lamp that we could have worn on our caps while 'coon hunting and the electric eye that would magically open windows and doors. We didn't learn the secrets of the pyramids, the mysteries of sex, or any secret Masonic rituals. Nor did we take advantage of the many opportunities to become popular, muscular, and irresistible to the opposite sex. No one ever laughed when we sat down to play the piano and stayed to stare in amazement as we became the life of the party. We never took the Charles Atlas courses that would have prevented big bullies from kicking sand in our face at the beach. We didn't learn to catch like Joe DiMaggio, walk and talk like the movie stars, or learn the secrets of how to marry the girl of our dreams. Instead, those long winter days, we read and reread the wish books and pulpy country magazine ads and dreamed on.

We spent many recesses poring over the colorful "funny papers" Mr. Twist gave us, fascinated by the mean little Katzenjammer boys, who threw hives of hornets and pots of glue and gave hot foots to the Captain and the Inspector. We suffered with Little Orphan Annie, and I secretly hoped that Dick Tracy, the big bully whom I hated, would be gunned down by one of the crooks he always caught. We learned a great deal about medieval history from Prince Valiant, space travel from Buck Rogers, and airplanes from Captain Jack. Lots of new words entered our vocabulary from the funnies. "Yowsah," "swell," "Kiddo," "yeah, man," "righto," "O.K.," and "rustle your bustle" colored our conversation and, we thought, made us rather sophisticated. Our teachers felt otherwise, however, and forbade such "vulgar" expressions in class, but all such little fads helped pass the long days of being shut in.

By the end of January, people always began to talk about Midwinter Day, an unofficial holiday invented as a milestone to indicate that winter was half over. February 2, which was Groundhog Day in the warmer parts of the country, had long ago been designated as our Midwinter Day. We were familiar with the groundhog legend and knew that the sleepy old fellow was supposed to come out of his burrow and blink a few times. If he saw his shadow, there would be six more weeks of winter. Since no Vermont woodchuck would leave his warm home and burrow up through four feet of snow to take a look around, we knew this tale was nonsense. Even if he did suffer from insomnia and were to do such a foolish thing in early February, we would certainly have ten more weeks of winter, no matter what he saw.

Midwinter Day was the time to take stock. We had to check the school's firewood to see if it were more than half gone. We examined our woodpile at home, too, and took inventory of our other supplies. Had the potatoes, carrots, turnips, maple syrup, canned goods, dried apples, and vinegar shrunk by more than half? Were the piles of hay, sawdust, corn, and oats below the halfway mark?

Although we usually had plenty of the critical items, sometimes life had to be adjusted after our inventory. We might need to sell a cow or two if feed was short, or, if we had plenty of fodder, it might be a good time to pick up a cow cheap. We might find more potatoes and apples and less maple syrup on the table for the next few weeks. Pessimism helped us survive, since there was no good way to tell exactly when spring would come. Possibly we would be digging parsnips in late April, and maybe we could let the cattle out to pasture in mid-May, but probably not.

The temperature always kept us on our toes, and we had

to keep an eye on a lot of different things. Some winters everything froze time after time, including drains, the water pipes, water tubs, manure pile, and doors. Kettles of water were kept hot for thawing things, and hot freestones were kept handy on the back of the stove. Even so, occasionally we had to borrow a blowtorch from the Cheevers.

Most winters, tons of heavy snow had to be shoveled off the roofs after each big storm. I helped my brothers clean off not only the house and barn but also the chicken house, milk house, two woodsheds, the ice house, garage, toolshed, pig house, and a small shop. We had to keep in mind, too, the sugarhouse, which was three-quarters of a mile away down in the woods in front of our house, and the little shed covering the spring, a quarter mile in the opposite direction. All the roofs were covered with cedar shingles or tar paper, so the snow never slid off by itself. We had to be especially careful not to break the fragile old shingles when we shoveled the snow or chopped the ice that often formed near the eaves.

Small wonder we rejoiced at learning winter was at last half over. With February came more holidays at school. We heard a great deal of moralizing about both Lincoln and Washington as their birthdays approached. We usually drew a few log cabins before Lincoln's Birthday and cut out hatchets and cherry trees to commemorate Washington's, pasting them as best we could to the frosty windows.

Valentine's Day was observed mostly as an art project rather than as a sentimental holiday, and it was much more appreciated by the girls than by the boys. Although we boys didn't enjoy the cutting, coloring, and pasting, we were forced each year to make valentines for our teacher and for everyone else in school. We created hearts and cupids from scraps of colored paper and wallpaper catalogues brought from home, and one year someone gave us a decal set. We had a wonderful time with that, soaking the colorful hearts, cupids, and flowers in water and sliding them off to decorate our valentines, lunch boxes, and windows.

My first year in school I didn't know what a valentine

was and was reluctant to print "Be My Valentine" on hearts addressed to my classmates. I was also very confused when I received them. This feeling persisted throughout my school years, and even in eighth grade, when I received a card that said, "Be Mine!" I felt uncomfortable.

Every year on February 14 each of us dutifully stuffed our creations into a brightly decorated box the teacher had made and waited as two appointed little "cupids" passed them out. We enjoyed the hour off from lessons and eagerly ate the cookies the teacher had brought, then took the hearts and flowers home for our family to admire.

After Midwinter Day, the walk home from school was usually slightly warmer than the morning hike. Although home was a warm oasis, it was seldom a hot one. Our house was in a windy spot, and some days it was impossible to keep it comfortably warm in spite of three roaring stoves. Uncle Peter used to say that Santa Claus could have ridden a tail-wind all the way from the North Pole and stopped at our house first!

Like every farm home, ours was filled with various aromas in spite of the winter winds blowing through the cracks. I often stepped through the doorway after my walk from school to the delicious fragrance of fresh fried doughnuts or newly baked bread, but intermingled were the not-so-pleasant scents of horse blankets drying, the frozen cornmeal and skim-milk slop thawing in the pig buckets, and smelly barn clothes being kept warm. During the evening the kerosene lights had a strong, oily smell, too.

My mother insisted on certain aspects of civilization, so even if our home had its share of country smells, it was never as wild or as interesting as the Markres home, which I was allowed to visit one wintry night. They had taken a box of newly hatched chicks and a newborn calf into the kitchen to keep them warm. Guns and animal traps hung from the walls, and fox skins were stretched out to dry behind the enormous stove, along with buffalo robes and huge amounts of winter clothing. Even the north wind didn't obliterate the resulting scent that was still attached to my clothes and hair when I arrived home.

Although I believed many of the old-timers' recollections, I strongly suspected prevarication when my uncles and aunts said they really enjoyed winter in the old days. They described enthusiastically the sleigh rides of their youth, singing and laughing on crisp starry nights as they dashed through newly fallen snow with cheeks glowing, hi-ing off to oyster suppers, card parties, and Grange plays. Their memories were probably faulty, I reasoned. Getting from home to anywhere and back in winter always required an abnormal effort.

I do not remember ever singing or laughing as we dashed through the snow on a sleigh or pung, our boxlike, one-horse sled. It always seemed to be extraordinarily cold when we took such a trip. Old Molly was always chosen to pull the sleigh, since she was the only horse we had that would drive well single and would run. Tucked under buffalo robes and coarse woolen brown blankets that reeked of horse sweat and mothballs, I peered out to see the white frost forming on the horse's hair and the sleigh and felt it gather on my own nose and ears. The soapstones we took along quickly chilled, as did my feet, hands, and finally, it seemed, my bone marrow. The rhythm of my chattering teeth seemed to keep time with that of the trotting horse, and her iron-shod hooves picked up blobs of cold snow and hurled them unerringly into my frozen face.

Before the town began to scrape the snow from the roads with a crawler tractor, they were packed after each snowfall with big wooden rollers. Often, while I was walking to school, I would meet the one that went over our roads, and, to a small boy, they were enormous and exciting. The roller consisted of two giant barrels side by side, held together by a massive frame that supported both an axle for the barrels and a seat on top for two drivers. Four horses hauled the contrivance, which moved quite easily on the level but needed lots of power to get up a steep hill in soft snow.

The roller's function was to compress the snow, which it

did, somewhat; but until several teams and sleds had been over the road to pack it hard, it was difficult to walk over it. By the end of the winter, sometimes more than eight feet of accumulated snow would be packed solidly in the road. In the spring we knew it would melt slowly, and a great deal of water would soak into the dirt, making it a mass of deep mud. We'd have to walk in the fields and pastures on the way to school and would often meet teams and automobiles also avoiding the road.

Riding the roller was a cold job. Usually the drivers were so bundled up in scarfs, sheepskins, and robes that only their eyes, noses, and pipes were visible, and you were never sure who they were. The roller that packed the roads on the west side of town had a little house on it to protect the drivers, but the one in our neighborhood was wide open, so the men perched high in the air caught all the wind.

The roller left a high ridge of unpacked snow in the middle of the road where the frame supported the two barrels, so the road looked like a divided highway. Since neither side was wide enough for a horse-drawn sled, the first one over it had to break through the barrier.

Naturally we couldn't use our car during the winter on the rolled roads; and we didn't use the sleigh much either, except for necessary trips such as meeting the doctor who'd driven as far as he could on the main road, for going to a funeral in the village, to town meeting, or to visit ailing Aunt Bessie. Our trips to town for provisions were made with a double sled and a team of horses.

When I was nearly through grade school, the town began to scrape the roads, and everyone was excited because we would no longer be snowbound all winter. They all quickly learned that driving in winter was quite different from doing so in summer, however. Starting out was the first chore, and extra time had to be allowed, since no car started well in cold weather. Our neighbors devised a heap of different ways to encourage their lazy vehicles. One man tore out a few stalls in his barn and kept his car next to his cattle.

Another put a wood stove in his garage. Most filled up their radiators with hot water before starting out, and some drew out the oil as soon as they got home and kept it warm in the house until they started out again. Jean Lapointe always put a pan of hot coals from the stove under his car for a few minutes, and Joe Waugh put a burning lantern beneath his vehicle and packed loose hay all around it. Since he kept his car in the haybarn, all his neighbors expected every day to see his place go up in smoke, but as far as I know, his method served him well.

Standard equipment for our winter drives included a shovel or two, tire chains, a putty knife to scrape the windshield, a bucket of sand, blankets to cover both the radiator and the passengers, and extra clothes for the walk home if we got stuck.

Every winter trip was fraught with adventure. We always put on the chains to start out but took them off as soon as we reached the main road, which was often bare and would quickly wear out the chains. On the way home my brothers could never resist the temptation to try to go as far as possible on the snow-covered roads without them. Invariably, after only a few minutes, we all had to shovel out the car and put on the chains in a ditch.

We tried to plan any trip out so we would not meet the milk truck, the mailman, or the people going to work. The science of scraping roads was not perfected, so they were never scraped wide enough at the beginning of the winter to leave room for all the snow that would fall throughout the rest of the season. By February the roads became extremely narrow, and if two drivers met, one of them had to back to a driveway or turnout, sometimes for a mile or more and often up or down a steep hill.

Some farmers decided it wasn't worth the trouble to drive with one hand and scrape the frost off the windshield with the other and cope with a balky car, frozen radiator, and bad battery. They "put their car up" for the winter just as they had done before the scraping began. Hiram Forge said that he figured the only excuse for winter was to let a body "set down with his whole heft for a few weeks," and, by dander, he planned to do just that.

I used to hear a lot about the Tuttles, who had their own special way with winter. They had lived in the woods behind our farm but had moved away long before I was born. Each fall the three Tuttle boys and their parents were said to have loaded up their buttery with enough flour, tobacco, and tea for winter, and the entire family didn't appear again until spring. According to the stories, since their cows were dry all winter and the chickens didn't lay eggs, the Tuttles woke up only once in the middle of each day and stayed awake just long enough to feed and water the animals and cook themselves a light lunch. Then they crawled back into bed and let the fire go out. They had no road, no visitors, never got any mail, and had no water pipes to freeze. Each year they hibernated for four months, and then, like the black bears, they woke up on a warm day in early April rarin' to go. They made lots of maple sugar, tore rapidly through their spring work, and still had time to "hire out" to the other neighbors who were more than glad to make use of all their energy.

I liked a lot of things about a Vermont winter, but there were many days when I wondered if the woodchucks, bears, and Tuttles didn't understand best how to handle it.

BUZZING BEES

When I was ten years old, the Campbells, a family that lived across town, invited my family to help out at a linoleum laying on a Saturday afternoon in winter. About twenty people, including the children, appeared for the event. The linoleum lay in a big roll in the corner of the empty living room, and since it measured nine feet by twelve feet and was to be laid in a room about twelve feet by fifteen feet, it seemed to me that we had plenty of help.

The grown-ups talked a great deal, so much that I was beginning to wonder if they had forgotten about the linoleum, but they finally tackled the project. Everyone got in one another's way as they laid down layers of newspapers to cover the wide cracks between the floor boards, rolled out the linoleum, and painstakingly straightened it. Finally, everyone was satisfied that it looked well-nigh perfect and pronounced it absolutely beautiful. The installation had taken more than an hour.

After the men had moved the furniture back into the room, the women carried in huge platters of sandwiches, large cakes with thick frostings, double-layered cookies with raspberry filling, and sweet raised doughnuts, as well as pitchers of coffee and milk. We all ate heartily. Then, after the dishes were whisked away, we children played Parcheesi while the older folks started a card game called 500. In late afternoon, as twilight darkened the sky, we bundled up and went home.

The afternoon was pleasant, but it was puzzling to me. Everyone there must have realized that one man could have rolled out that piece of linoleum in fifteen minutes. I didn't comprehend then that their strong work ethic would not have allowed rational Yankees and Scots to get together simply to eat and play games, even on a blustery winter weekend. There had to be a legitimate excuse, and a "bee" provided it nicely.

Our own little neighborhood didn't have as many work bees as some other rural areas. The Yankee farmers were very independent and didn't enjoy working closely with their neighbors. They felt that the Lord helped those who helped themselves, and most could afford to think that way since they had families large enough to handle their own work. We held a bee only for a big job like sawing the woodpile, cutting ice, threshing oats, or putting up a new barn or silo.

Our neighbors on the west side of town were quite different. They were far more sociable and were likely to get together at the slightest excuse. They assembled not only to lay linoleum but also to clean a chimney, patch a roof, make cider, or cut the horns off their cows, none of which actually required a crowd of people. The women rallied for the traditional quilting bee as well as for making jelly, papering a room, shelling peas, or making applesauce.

One of the times our neighborhood worked together was to get the summer's supply of ice. Cutting ice was not as involved or long lasting a job as "getting up" a woodpile or cutting lumber for a new toolshed, but it was hard, cold work. A group of men assembled for the cutting, and each, afterward, hauled his own requirements to his farm.

The farmers in northern Vermont had recently switched from selling cream to whole milk. Since cream was soured before being churned into butter, no refrigeration had been necessary. Milk, on the other hand, had to be quickly cooled each day, so every farm had been required to buy an insulated tank to hold the ice and water necessary for cooling.

Each February, as soon as the ice was thick enough, the men in our neighborhood broke a road through the snow in the woods to Long Pond, about a mile away from our home.

Two or three feet of snow usually had to be shoveled off the ice, which was then sawed by hand into cubes about fifteen inches on each side. My brothers drew ours home in a two-horse sled and packed it into our new ice house. Each layer was carefully covered with several inches of fresh sawdust that had been hauled from the village sawmill.

Since the ice-cutting operation usually took place when I was in school and lasted for only four or five years—until we got electricity—I went only once on the ice trip to Long Pond. My job was to watch the horses, since I was too small to help out with the cutting. The ice was extremely slippery, and I was warned frequently not to get too close to the operation. Although the men wore sharp metal creepers on their boot heels to keep them from slipping, each year we heard of someone falling into the cold water while hauling out the heavy, crystal-clear cubes with ice tongs.

During ice week a great deal of traffic went past our house. Sometimes I caught a ride home from school on an empty sled going to the pond for a last load. One day the Coomer brothers, three rugged farmer-woodsmen, came along with their rig and invited me aboard. The boys were always nice to me, although many of our neighbors were wary of them because they drank heavily, swore violently, and looked wild and unkempt. They were wearing heavy leather coats, gauntlet gloves, and heavy black hip boots, and all were chewing tobacco, talking loud, and grinning through their brown-stained teeth.

I stood at the back of the sled, playing with their yellow dog, which always trotted behind. As we started down the long, steep hill toward home, I forgot to hang on. For some reason the horses stopped suddenly, as did the sled, the dog, and the three Coomers—everyone but me. I fell down and slid the entire length of the long sled, now very slippery from the ice chips, bowling over one Coomer after another along the way. We all landed at the front of the sled in a heap of rubber, leather, chewing tobacco, and strong-smelling human flesh. Unfortunately, I was very near the bottom of the heap.

Len, who had been driving, dropped the reins in the excitement. The horses decided that that was a signal to get going, which they did, at a lively clip down the hill. To add to the excitement, the dog started to bark furiously.

It took quite some time to get the horses slowed down, the dog shut up, and everyone untangled and upright in the slippery sled. Unfortunately the Coomers failed to see the humor of the situation, and I picked up several new obscenities and some fascinating combinations of the mouth-soaping words I already knew. Since I was at fault, it seemed like good judgment to get off at the first chance and walk the rest of the way home. I tried to avoid meeting the Coomers for the next few weeks.

Besides using ice for cooling milk, a fringe benefit of having it on hand all summer was that we acquired a home-made icebox for the first time. My brother-in-law had constructed the box out of lumber, made an inner lining of sheet metal, and packed about six inches of sawdust between the two for insulation. We drilled a hole in the floor of a back room as a drain for the melting ice, installed the box, and began to store our butter, vegetables, and milk there instead of in the cellar. On very special Sundays we mixed some of the ice with rock salt in a crank-type freezer and made ice cream.

The annual January thaw was traditionally the time for butchering. Although no one understood the phenomenon, invariably, after several weeks of bitter cold the weather suddenly became warm for two or three days, and it was possible to work bare-handed. Since no one knew for sure when the thaw would come, everything had to be ready well ahead of time.

Nearly every Yankee was a big meat eater, and each farmer fattened one or two large hogs and a beef each winter for his family's use. Some towns had a semi-professional butcher who did the job for the less skillful farmers, but in our neck of the woods, most either tried to do it themselves or got together with a few neighbors. Butchering together, they could get the operation completed at one time, use the same equipment, and take advantage of one another's expertise. Like so many other farm jobs, it was a once-a-year chore, so most men never got very good at it. Fred Cheever usually brought his two pigs to our house each year in a big box on a sled and butchered them with ours.

Fortunately, in our school we were always discouraged from staying home to work, unless there was a real emergency. At butchering time I was always glad to be in school so I didn't have to help with the smelly, messy job. Occasionally the thaw came on a Saturday, however, and my job was to keep the fire going, carry water, and that sort of thing. A lot of hot water was needed to scald the dead hogs, so before sunrise we had to start the fire and carry a good many pails of water to fill the big pan. Everyone wore his oldest overalls and rolled up his high rubber boots before tackling the wet job.

Butchering, in my opinion, was the only job worse than cleaning out the barn basement in the spring. The high-pitched squealing of the pigs was discomfiting as they were thrown on their backs and had their throats slit. I disliked the struggle with the cow as she was led from her warm stall through the wet, mushy snow, protesting all the way, and I did not enjoy seeing her drop slowly down after the sharp, loud shot. I didn't like walking through the snow that was covered for days with blood, entrails, and bristles, nor did I like the putrid odor of the boiling water in the big scalding tub as the pigs were repeatedly pulled high in the air by pulley blocks and dunked to soften their tough hair so it could be scraped smooth.

Even with many people working on the job, it was two or three days before the meat was cut up and frozen by nature in a back room, the sausage made, the lard melted, and the salt pork and hams pickled in brine in large stoneware tubs. Later in the winter we took the hams from the cellar and smoked them slowly in a covered barrel by burning corncobs and maple bark under them. A small amount of snow had to be added to the fuel from time to time to prevent the fire from blazing up and cooking the meat. To get them properly smoked took all day, and it was usually a Saturday job for me.

The most important annual work bees in our neighborhood were the firewood sawings. Seven to ten able-bodied men were needed to operate the machine that sawed the big pile of hardwood logs every family cut each winter into short lengths for firewood. For two or three weeks the equipment was moved from farm to farm, and usually each man worked at several places. Most workers enjoyed the camaraderie as well as the big holiday-type dinners the womenfolk provided.

The arrival of the sawing machine in our yard was an exciting event. I loved machinery of all kinds, and it was fun to try to figure out how the noisy contraption worked. It was brought in on a sled by a team of horses and consisted of two parts: the saw rig, which was large and bulky, but not too heavy; and the engine, a smaller but extremely heavy black monster made by Fairbanks-Morse. It had two enormous flywheels, an oiler on the top, and one giant-sized piston, and when it was started up, it made one heck of a racket.

We usually had to move a great deal of snow to make room for the saw rig before it arrived, and several men and lots of levers were needed to get it into place. The back-and-forth movement of the piston rotated the flywheels, which drove another pulley by way of a belt. This pulley had a cam and another shaft on it that converted the rotary motion of the wheel back into a to-and-fro movement that made the saw go back and forth like a large handsaw. A great deal of vibration was created, so the whole thing had to be well anchored with wooden stakes that were pounded into the frozen ground.

The day after the machine was set up, the crew arrived. Each man did a particular job, usually the one he liked best, but there was some swapping around during the day. The sawyer Mr. Finney, who owned the machine, was top man. He worked the levers and foot pedals that put the saw in motion, kept it in place on the log, and raised and lowered it with a collection of pulleys, counterweights, and clutches. He was also the saw sharpener, and sometimes he appointed someone to take his place at the machine while he took a saw into the kitchen and sharpened it with a file.

One or two men rolled down the logs from the pile. They had to be careful not to let the heavy logs get away from them and crash into the men or machine at the bottom. The log being sawed rested on a little carriage that sat on two metal-covered wooden tracks. After each cut, another man shoved the log up for the next cut. Two men held the log in place with levers that had spikes in them. Although this job was the easiest, and about all one had to do was stay awake, it was also the coldest, and on a raw, cold day no one wanted to do it. Two more men took the sawed blocks away from the machine and rolled them into a pile. Sometimes, if there was enough help, another man split the larger chunks into smaller pieces. Taking away the blocks and piling them was considered the lowest on the job scale and was the task we kids were likely to get if the sawing was done on a Saturday, when we were home from school.

Conversation was impossible above the noise of the machine. You could talk to the person next to you only if you yelled loudly. The engine didn't fire at every revolution of the big wheels, only when it needed to in order to keep the thing running. An ingeniously conceived governor arranged the firing according to the load the engine was bearing, and the sound ranged from a *bang-chug-chug-chug-chug-bang*, when the engine was idling, to *bang-chug-bang-bang-chug-bang-bang-bang-chug* when it was grinding through a tough maple log. After an hour's sawing, the water in the radiator boiled furiously, even on a cold day, and the engine produced clouds of white steam as well as smoke and noise.

By noon everyone was hungry and looked forward to a big meal. Mountains of potatoes, meat, squash, baked beans, turnips, pickles, and pies disappeared as the crowd of hungry men tossed aside their Sunday manners and dug in.

The women in the family never ate with the men on this

occasion but trotted the food into the dining room from the kitchen with a great sense of pride at the relish with which the results of their hard work were being consumed. Surprisingly, I never heard my mother complain about the vast quantities of snow tracked over her freshly scrubbed floors.

No matter how good the meal or how blustery the day, at one o'clock the men gave a quick tug to the wide belt that cranked the engine, and the afternoon's work began. "Many hands make light work," someone would always say when they got together for a difficult job, and at least once each day someone would have to remove his gloves to do some tinkering. "Cat can't catch mice with mittens on," he would invariably remark, to which a heavily clad companion always replied, "Make a damn good try when it's 40 below."

Although sawing wood, butchering, or cutting ice was hard work, at the end of the day the men seemed surprisingly happy. Most of the farmers in our neighborhood didn't belong to any organization, and their life was tedious and lonely. For many, a work bee was their only social life outside the family all winter.

TEACHERS AND THEIR TRIALS

We didn't get a new teacher very often, as it was considered proper for a schoolmarm to stay at least two years in each school. Some did not stay with us that long, however, and one year we had three. While most of our teachers had two years of training at what was called a Normal School, one very young girl who had gone for only one year decided after a couple of weeks that teaching was not for her. Another, after a month, was excused by the school board for lack of discipline.

Our teachers were paid fifteen dollars each week. They boarded at various farms in the neighborhood and usually walked to school. The Finneys' was a favorite boarding place, even though, like the rest of us, they had no electricity. Occasionally one stayed with the Cheevers, who lived on a hill, and they had no running water, either. New teachers from more civilized areas must have been dedicated to teaching to be willing to pump their water, heat it on the stove, and walk a mile to school on rainy and wintry days.

It was both exciting and frustrating for us to get a new teacher. We wondered not only whether she would be nice or mean but also how long it would take to train her to abide by all the comfortable old traditions that guided our lives.

Each new teacher, naturally, had a mind of her own and never seemed impressed when we pointed out that we had never done things her way before. We grudgingly moved the furniture around for Miss Perrin when she decided she could better watch her charges with her desk positioned at the back of the room. Two weeks later she had us move it all back to its original position, just as we knew she would.

Another teacher, Miss Goodrich, felt we should have warm cocoa with our cold box lunch every day during the winter. Unfortunately, her idea didn't last long, either. Washing dishes with no running water was a problem, as was heating the milk over the wood stove without scalding it.

The year I was in seventh grade, Miss Reynolds conducted a humiliating experiment. Far ahead of her time, she felt that every girl should learn to use a hammer, saw, screwdriver, and paintbrush, and each boy should learn to knit, crochet, and sew on buttons. The girls had a wonderful time making crooked bookends and pot-holder hangers. We boys, however, bitterly resented the "sissy" work, especially when she made us do it as we recited at the front of the room. Most of us finally got the knack of buttons, but our crocheted productions looked even worse than the girls' bookends. I never came close to figuring out knitting, nor did I intend to.

This same progressive teacher redeemed herself in our eyes, however, by buying a set of encyclopedias with her own meager salary. She put them on the shelf for us to use in our spare time, and the older pupils, hungry for information, spent hours looking at the pictures and reading all sorts of exciting things. Through them we gained a passing knowledge of terms like "relativity" and "atoms" several years before they became household words. They were the only new books in the school.

In spite of their brave tries, most teachers found, sooner or later, that things went best when they were done the way they always had been. Even so, we dreaded the annual state teachers' conventions and hoped that "just this year" ours would decide not to go. Invariably, however, they went, stayed two days, and came back fired with new-fangled ideas about how to best funnel extra knowledge into pupils' heads. For about two weeks, although it always seemed much longer, we suffered through the second-hand efforts of John Dewey and his crusading disciples. We acted out historical events, made up workbooks, researched projects and wrote them up, and otherwise performed "learning experiences." The experts had never programmed these activities for an eight-grade school, however, and the teachers found that they had no time to make them workable. Gradually they were abandoned, and our life returned to dull, comfortable normalcy, at least until the next convention or the next new teacher.

Although our school had an impressive number of rules, the dos and don'ts were not posted or written anywhere. We were all expected to know what was permissible, what was frowned on, and what was considered a serious offense. In the classroom it was forbidden to walk around without permission or to make any kind of noise. It was wrong to write on the walls, wear your cap in school, talk with your mouth full at lunch, or fight in the schoolyard. And on and on.

One problem our teachers had to cope with was swearing. Some children heard it at home continually, and most of us were so naive we were not sure which words were forbidden and which were only slang and therefore still permissible. We found it risky to try out the new expressions we had read in dime novels or learned from the older boys. I was always surprised by the teacher's quick judgment and wondered how she acquired her vast knowledge of all those words.

Mrs. Marshall decided to treat swearing in the old-fashioned way by popping a cake of soap into the offender's mouth and making him rinse it out with water. Some of the boys blew lots of bubbles the year of her tenure.

Steve Markres, who sat in back of Molly Forge, was bothered one day by her long pigtails flopping over his desk and cut one of them off with his new pocketknife. Molly was in tears and the teacher was visibly upset, unsure of what punishment could possibly fit such a deed. Molly's parents were not at all happy about it, either. We boys secretly thought it was hilarious, and since Steve was part Indian, we said he had no doubt yielded to the Iroquois instinct to scalp somebody.

Steve spent all his recesses in his seat for two weeks thinking it over.

That was the punishment that hurt us most—keeping us in our seats at recess—and everybody was disciplined this way at one time or another. Our teachers didn't believe that one guilty person should ever go unpunished, even if it meant locking up the entire school whenever they weren't sure who'd closed the pipe damper on the furnace and filled the schoolhouse with smoke, or who'd tied a hard knot in Rose Barker's coat sleeve.

Although our teachers never used a dunce cap, they used the other traditional punishments and made us put our heads down on our desks or stand in a corner. Miss Goodrich told Aaron Jillson that he would grow up with a three-cornered head because he was in the corner so often. Aaron had so much energy that sitting still or keeping quiet was practically impossible for him. He was expert at making faces and at playing tricks on everybody, including the teacher. The rest of us couldn't resist retaliating and usually got caught. One day when a mousetrap bomb I had rigged up for him made more noise than I expected, I had to stay after school and write, "I wasted time in school today" fifty times on the blackboard. (The teacher felt that good paper shouldn't be wasted on rehabilitation.)

Fortunately only one teacher in my years at school believed that to spare the rod was to spoil the child. A very nervous person, she became easily excited over what we considered minor infractions, and during her blessedly short tenure, we all got several beatings. Her punishments ranged from a sharp crack on the knuckles with a heavy two-foot ruler to a bottoms-up beating over a desk with a rubber hose. We always yelled "bloody murder" hoping it would help, but she showed no mercy. If corporal punishment was against the law, she was completely unaware of it, and so were we.

The long-standing neighborhood rule was that if we got a licking at school, we always got another, harsher punishment at home. Although this didn't always happen, parents did find out via the grapevine everything that happened at school. The day we boys got a thrashing for drawing a picture of the teacher on the blackboard when she was out of the room, all of our parents knew it before we got home.

We were all warned frequently by our elders about a sinister character called the truant officer. According to the reports, he apparently liked nothing better than to grab an errant child and lock him up in a terrible place called the reform school until he was twenty-one years old. None of us ever saw the truant officer, but we understood him to be some sort of hybrid between Simon Legree and Bluebeard, an image that kept us from acting any worse than we did.

We felt lucky that he never appeared—the district superintendent was frightening enough. At least twice each year he made a visit to our school. Sometimes in the spring or fall when the front door was open, he'd slip in quietly, and we'd look up, surprised and alarmed to find him standing there observing the proceedings. He was a tall, stern-looking man with beady eyes, a mustache, and a deep bass voice that terrified us all. He never lectured us, though, and it was probably the teacher, rather than we, who was on trial during his visits, but we were always on our best behavior when he was there. On these occasions, the teachers often, on the spur of the moment, asked "review" questions about lessons we already knew well, and this made both her and us look pretty favorable.

Sometimes a state helping teacher, always a woman, surprised us with a visit, too. As a rule she seemed satisfied if we could read and write, and she became only moderately upset if we pronounced Chile, New Delhi, and Worcester the way they looked. Her visits were blessedly short, and we always had the feeling that she couldn't get back to the civilized world of Montpelier fast enough.

Most of our teachers were country girls themselves, but Miss Demars came from a large town. She never showed much fondness for the backwoods and found the local smells particularly foul, which surprised me. When I went to town,

I hadn't found the scent of coal smoke, cigars, and gasoline very delightful, either. Throughout her year with us, we would often see her wrinkle her nose and murmur something unflattering about fresh country air.

Some boys came directly from the barn to school without changing their clothes or boots, and even a two-mile hike in a brisk wind didn't erase the evidence of their homework, especially in winter, when all the windows had to be closed.

Because water was so limited, winter was not a time of great cleanliness in certain homes. Jim Temple told us in a matter-of-fact way that he took a bath at least once every month during the summer but he didn't take them quite as often in the winter. Although probably no one was sewn into long johns in the method described in country legends, certain folks were encouraged by their cold homes to sleep in their clothes. After weeks without washing, the resulting aroma added to the general lived-in scent of the school.

Salt pork, potatoes, and baked beans were a mainstay of winter diets in many homes, and the resulting bouquet was offensive to everyone's olfactory system. Raw onion sandwiches seemed to be one of the favorite lunchpail treats for some pupils, and they were not encouraged to linger long when they went to the teacher's desk for help.

Although spring was always welcomed after the confining winter atmosphere, it offered little respite to our unfortunate teacher's nose. When she threw open the windows on the first warm day in anticipation of some relief from the winter odors, she found the adjoining farmers spreading manure on both fields surrounding our school. It was not a pleasant day for her, but even our well-acclimated country noses were aware of the potent, steamy cow, pig, and horse manure that had fermented in a basement under the barn all winter.

Probably the sniff that burst the endurance cell in Miss Demars's nostrils came in the spring when we boys went into the Tylers' maple woods one lunch hour and ate a generous helping of newly sprouted leeks. Certain we had eaten the wild garlic only to cause her grief, she kept us after school, lamenting our lack of consideration and steadfastly refusing to believe that we had done it on a dare. We tried to assure her that we liked her and didn't at all enjoy eating the powerful herbs.

I hope that Miss Demars's sensitive nose enjoyed the scent of maple syrup boiling in April; the fresh, thawing earth in May; the apple and lilac blossoms in June; green woods and clear running streams in summer; the newly fallen leaves in October; and the clear, crisp air on February days. If she noticed them, they were apparently not enough. She decided that fifteen dollars a week was not worth it and didn't sign her contract for a second year. We were sorry to see one of our favorite teachers leave us. The last we heard of her, she was downcountry, somewhere near Boston, possibly enjoying the smell of oil refineries, chemical plants, and spoiling fish.

Another trial for our teachers was the subject that in most schools was considered delightful—singing. Music, unfortunately, was not a big thing in our tone-deaf neighborhood, and, except for our one French-Canadian family, I seldom heard anyone sing or play an instrument. Fiddlers for dances were imported, and singing, outside of school, was limited mostly to drunks trying to find their way home late at night.

We received no formal music lessons, but because most teachers felt that some sort of instruction was essential to a proper education, singing was a ritual, not only at Halloween and Christmas programs but also frequently at morning exercises as well. The fact that almost no one in the entire school could sing deterred the teachers very little. Armed with a pitchpipe and the wheezy old organ, they aimed to change things. We *would* learn to sing.

Luckily, one girl in the entire school was not tone deaf and could actually carry a tune. It was Isabel Tootson's duty to hold our mournful little chorus together. She could never remember the words, unfortunately, so she sang a melodic "Yah, yah, yah," while the rest of us supplied the words.

Our failure to carry a tune bothered us very little, for we didn't know what good singing was. Most of us had never heard any, since we didn't hear the summer concerts in the village or the traveling choruses that came to Hardwick. Radios in the neighborhood were filled with static, and the old phonographs were raspy and scratchy.

One day Roger Lincoln's dog followed him to school, and, since it was a warm spring morning, the door was open. The dog wandered in unnoticed during morning exercises and sat quietly by the stove. When we started to sing, the dog joined in. Teacher seemed to hesitate before chasing him out. She probably felt that Bozo sounded a lot better than we did.

Urged on by our teachers, we persisted, singing badly and loudly. At school programs the audience frequently joined in on the familiar songs, hoping, no doubt, to drown us out. That helped very little, however, since very few adults in our neighborhood could sing either.

One day Charlie Forge brought his cousin to school with him. The stranger was about eleven years old, visiting from another town. When we started to sing "America the Beautiful," he sang, too—loudly, on key, clear as a bell, and beautifully. We all stopped to listen. None of us had ever heard anything like that, and we were in awe. I wish I could say that after his visit we all sang better, but the talent simply didn't exist. We realized for the first time how terrible we sounded, and from then on we hated to sing in public. It suddenly became all too obvious to us what our teachers had long known. If we were to make a name for ourselves in this world, it was not going to be as a Kate Smith or Rudy Vallee.

Even though our teachers failed miserably as singing instructors, they taught us to read and write, master decimals and division, appreciate poetry, history, and geography, and they even drummed in some manners and morals to boot. How they mustered up that much patience, I'll never understand.

NEVER LOOK FOR THE
SILVER LINING

Whenever Rose and Lily Barker came to school and reported a case of smallpox in the village, an arsonist loose, or that their father had just seen a cockroach in Cuthberton's store, we never knew for sure whether to believe them. We did know, however, that it was our beholden duty to pass on the bad news promptly. It was not considered good form to be the last to report trouble.

If a neighbor returning from town announced that he had just heard some good news and some bad news, everyone wanted to hear the bad news first. People not only enjoyed bad news, but they also seemed especially happy to be among the first to report it. In the Depression years, we all desperately wanted to hear about someone who might be a bit worse off than we were.

Pessimism was a safe way to make any happening turn out better than we had hoped. After all, if you always expected the worst, it couldn't possibly be that bad. If someone was hurt by a horse, someone else was sure to predict, "He will probably die." When a child was born, very likely the baby would be reported as "too sickly to live." We expected crops to fail, barns to collapse, cows to abort, and banks to foreclose.

Trouble and hardship surrounded us, and we knew exactly how to handle them. Everyone I knew would rise magnanimously to the occasion when a neighbor's house burned, or there was a sudden accident, a death, or serious illness. The neighbors were all sympathetic and helpful.

But no one knew quite how to react to good news. Contrary to the maxim "Laugh and the world laughs with you, cry and you cry alone," most people in our neighborhood found it rather difficult to accept any sign of good fortune. An acquaintance who got a new car, bought a radio, sold a chunk of land at a high price, or inherited some money was likely to be talked about in rather unpleasant terms for years. "If he's so gol' 'ram much better than the rest of us, why, so far as we're concerned, he can just go and fry ice."

Optimism was not popular, whether you were considering your own prospects for success or your neighbor's. If a neighbor built an enormous barn and filled it chuckerblock full of hay, no one would ever tell him, "By crimus, you shore have built yourself quite a structure there." Instead, the proper reaction would be to look it over carefully for a few minutes and say, thoughtfully, "One stroke of lightning and you'd be out of business." He would think a while and remark, "Yup. Hay het and burned a barn just like this one over in Enosburg Falls last month. Flatter 'n a doorstone in twenty minutes."

Or if one pleasant morning a neighbor was found leaning on the fence watching his prosperous-looking herd of Jerseys as they ate their fill of clover, no Yankee ever said, "I snum, you must be hauling in money hand over fist." Instead, after looking over each animal carefully, your proper comment would be, "T.B. could wipe that herd right out in nothin' flat." He'd retort gloomily, "A-ya, and Bang's disease would be just as bad."

Because of everyone's pessimistic outlook, any new venture was not likely to be encouraged, so most people stayed safely within the status quo. Mark Coomer was an exception. One year he built a new silo and planted a large field of corn. Everyone predicted that he would wear out his soil quickly, the stuff would spoil, the cows would never eat it, and, if they did ingest silage, they would give smelly milk. The talk didn't worry Mark one bit, though. It was exactly what he'd expected. Although anyone from "away" would probably have been rather puzzled by the pessimistic attitude of the neighbors, it seemed perfectly normal to Mark, and to the rest of us.

Just as optimism was out of the question, praise was rarely given, and it was not expected. Praise was confusing, and it made a person suspicious. "Soft soap is 90 percent lye," pointed out Mrs. Forge one day when someone complimented her on her lush vegetable garden.

It was extremely important to keep adults, as well as children, "in their place" in our Yankee society. Men were careful not to compliment their wives, nor would wives commend their husbands. One might then begin to feel too good for his or her partner. The story about the Yankee who loved his wife so much it was all he could do to keep from telling her so might have originated in our neighborhood.

Telling a hired man he'd "done good" was too risky to chance, too. He'd probably want more pay, or would quit working for you and go right out and buy his own farm. Instead, a critical suggestion now and then was the recommended method of keeping his nose to the grindstone.

One of the local summer folk invited Arnold Rivers to Boston to see a Big League baseball game. Knowing that the old farmer had never left home, this person felt it was a good way to reward him for some favors he'd done, such as shoveling the cottage roof in winter and supplying him with wood and ice.

On the day of the big game, the farmer and the city banker sat under the blazing sun in the ballpark. Arnold appeared very attentive and chewed furiously as he observed the progress of the very tense game. In one critical play, an outfielder leaped high in the air and caught the ball. The thousands of spectators jumped to their feet in wild excitement—that is, everyone but Arnold, who sat completely unperturbed, never missing a chew on his cud of tobacco.

"Didn't you see that fellow catch the ball? demanded the city man."

"Shore."

"Well, didn't you think it was exciting?"

"Wal, no, not really. I figured that was what he was out there for."

In our world, you got no credit for doing what you were supposed to do.

Consequently, the teacher rarely told us that we had done our work well, because that was expected. Only our failings were likely to be pointed out. One day while walking to school, Roger Lincoln found a fat wallet beside the road. Finding Sam Traverse's name in it, he walked to the Rices' and called up the owner. Later in the day, Sam came to school and claimed the wallet. He gave Roger a nickel for a reward, but no thanks or praise. He'd done what he was supposed to, hadn't he?

My Yankee neighbors had a pessimistic outlook and were always eager to share it at every opportunity. One time Alpha Washburn mournfully described the building of his new tool shed. "It cost me a lot more than I thought it would," he said shaking his head solemnly, "but then I knowed it would."

FOLKS FROM AWAY

Visitors were rare in our area, and when they'd gone we talked about them for days afterward. Our area was off the beaten path, and life was slow, quiet, and dull. Everything moved slowly on the farm. Our speed was geared to that of the workhorse, about three miles an hour. The stillness was broken only now and then by an occasional car or truck and by farmers yelling at their horses or calling the cows. Cow calling was considered an art, and at milking time when the air was quiet we could hear callers in all directions, some a mile or two away. Each man was very proud of his "Come, Boss" and tried to outdo his neighbors both in volume and in quantity whether it was necessary or not. We could count on Hiram Forge to hold forth for fifteen minutes every night and morning, even when his cows were already waiting at the barn door.

Because of the boredom, we welcomed any change from our routine, either at home or at school.

One day, after morning exercises, our teacher told us that she had a surprise. However, instead of announcing that school had been canceled for the rest of the year, as we had hoped, she announced that in place of afternoon classes, she had invited Sue Johnson to give a talk about Washington. We all knew Sue slightly as the older daughter of one of the nearby farmers, but we seldom saw her since she had a job in Barre, thirty-five miles away. Any change from our school routine was welcome, however, so we looked forward to her visit.

Sue, who was about twenty-two years old, came into her former schoolroom after lunch, armed with a packet of booklets and colored picture postcards. She had lots of enthusiasm and soon swept us all into a travelogue I'll never forget. She had carefully saved up fifty dollars and bought a ticket for a train excursion to Washington, where she had spent an exciting week at cherry blossom time.

For the next three hours we sat, entranced, as she showed us her colored postcards of reflecting pools, monuments, huge buildings, and busy streets. She had seen Huey Long and Vice President Garner, sat where Abraham Lincoln had once sat, and been inside the theatre where he'd been shot. She had seen the Whispering Gallery, the White House, and the plane in which Charles Lindbergh had flown to Paris. She'd watched money being made in the U.S. mint, visited the Supreme Court, and seen the embassies of several foreign countries. She had ridden in a streetcar and, incredibly, had even watched Congress vote against one of President Roosevelt's pet measures. It was all so exciting that none of us complained about missing recess.

We talked about her visit for days. Someone we knew, a local woman, had actually gone to Washington and done the things we thought were possible only in books. Most of the people we knew had never traveled far beyond the village. Before Sue's visit none of us knew anybody who even knew anybody who had been to our nation's capital. To us, it had been as far removed as King Arthur's Camelot or Flash Gordon's Saturn. We now felt it might be possible for us to go away, too, and perhaps travel to such distant places as New York City, Cairo, or Bombay. Geography took on a new dimension and suddenly became more than a few dark, blurry pictures in our well-worn books.

Visitors to our own neighborhood were rare in the early 1930s, and whether we were in the house or barn, we always ran to the windows when a car went by. Sometimes the summer folks vacationing at the lake in the village drove along our road, looking for a place to fish, a landscape to paint, or perhaps some natives to observe, but they seldom spoke to us. Only occasionally did a passerby turn into our driveway and knock on the door.

Charlie Burwick, who peddled Raleigh products throughout the county, was our most regular visitor and stopped in about once a month when the roads were good. His truck held an amazing assortment of flavorings, drugs, salves, cosmetics, cleansers, and some packaged foods. Charlie was a fat, loud character with a none-too-subtle sales technique. He always opened the front door and bellowed, "How do you do!" in a deep, booming voice, whether we were in the far room or already in the process of opening the door. This procedure didn't go over well with everyone, and Mrs. Barker claimed she always made him step back outside, knock, and come in the way he was supposed to. Although my family bought only an occasional bottle of vanilla or liniment—and, once in two years, a jar of mentholated ointment—he always took a half hour or more to present his wares, and he concurrently dispensed lots of news.

Charlie, like the other peddlers, was viewed with mixed feelings. Everyone, male or female, felt a sense of isolation, and it was good to talk to someone outside the family once in a while, especially when they could bring in the doin's from outside. Still, there was an ever-present fear of letting unfamiliar folks into the house, especially peddlers. The suspicion was prevalent that every salesman was "out ta getcha," a feeling that had developed from experience.

The junkman came only once a year, to sell an assortment of kettles and pans and to collect rags, old automobile batteries, pieces of lead, copper pipe, and scraps of zinc. These were carefully picked from the junk we took to our farm dump by the brook each spring. Our junk man was small and wiry and had a strong accent. The Yankees never learned how to bargain successfully with him, so by the time he was gone we were ten or fifteen cents richer for our rags and scrap and considerably poorer for all the cheap tin pots and pans we had acquired.

We were visited occasionally by cattle traders, too. Some of them arrived in large trucks as if they planned to buy the whole herd. They wore pin-striped overalls, flat straw hats, and elastic armbands. They smoked long cigars and had dark blue checkbooks and pens sticking prominently out of their front pockets. As a rule, they were a loud-talking, unscrupulous bunch, and many back country farmers who trusted them got into deep debt because of their wheeling and dealing.

Fertilizer salesmen dropped in, too, and every few years a young man who was selling *New England Homestead, Country Gentleman,* or *American Agriculturist* came to our home. He always claimed to be working his way through college and usually had a "special" that included three years of the paper, plus a package of flower seeds or a picture "suitable for framing," for a dollar. If we subscribed, he would nail a metal sign with the magazine's name onto the barn or a nearby tree. He claimed that the sign would protect us from dishonest salesmen, though he never explained how. If we bought the paper, my brothers always took the sign down soon after he left, but one or two people in the neighborhood had the front doors of their barns covered with signs advertising different magazines, cream separators, and milking machines.

From time to time, a life insurance salesman or someone selling automobiles stopped at our home. The latter were by far the most pushy, because they had been well trained by the car companies. Also, they were native Vermonters and knew how to talk the farmer's language and capitalize on his fascination for the newfangled invention. So successful were they that many a seedy old Yankee suddenly owned a shiny new Ford or Chevy that he was not at all sure he wanted and hadn't the slightest idea how to drive or pay for.

A sewing machine repairman came by every few years to offer his services, and one day a man stopped in, wanting to sharpen our scissors and knives. Ma always suspected that these wayfarers were from one of the gypsy caravans that sometimes passed along the valley road in the summer, and she firmly refused to let any of them inside the house. My brothers delighted in telling me that the salesmen were out scouting the countryside for little boys for the gypsies to steal and would probably be back in a few days to get me. I knew they were joking, but for a couple of days after their visits, I half-expected to see men with gold earrings and large bags lurking behind the trees as I went to school.

Real, genuine tramps seldom passed through our neighborhood, since our locale was not considered an easy touch. The few times they came around, they created a lot of excitement, though, and the women with telephones carefully monitored the progress of each vagrant. Everyone breathed a sigh of relief when Grammy Johnson reported on the phone that she had just seen one of them pass around the curve beyond her place, headed north for Glover.

Although there was never any shortage of stories about violent robberies, murder, and arson committed by tramps who were denied a handout, I never heard of such an incident in our neighborhood. Most tramps seemed to be lazy, rather simple-minded men, and although they were dirty and bewhiskered, they never appeared dangerous, except in one way. We occasionally found evidence that one of these knights of the road had slept in our haybarn, which was always upsetting, because the matches and tobacco papers strewn around the next morning reminded us of the ever-present threat of fire.

Once the local constable tracked a mysterious character through the township for about a week. No one had gotten a good look at him, since he always darted into the woods when anyone approached. Late one evening the officer came by our house to ask if we had seen him. Then he asked one of my brothers if he would be willing to get up early the next morning and look in all the nearby abandoned buildings, barns, and sugar houses to see if the bum was sleeping in any of them.

About 4:30, just as it was getting light, my brother got up

and started sleepily to make the rounds when he suddenly realized that he had forgotten to ask the keeper of the law what he was supposed to do with the man if he found him. Obviously, there was no good way he could take him in if he didn't want to be taken, and, since he wasn't wanted dead or alive, he couldn't very well shoot him.

Fortunately the problem didn't come up. The man had already begun to make mysterious appearances in another town.

One spring during my schooldays, a man walked through the neighborhood every few days carrying a big suitcase. Sometimes he was going one way, and sometimes another. No one recognized him or knew what he was doing. All that season, until summer, the small children were made to stay close to the house, and we heard that some men kept loaded guns handy just in case the mystery man appeared. I wanted to stop him and ask who he was and what he was up to, but I wasn't allowed, because he might be dangerous. Besides, knowing the truth would have spoiled the mystery.

GOD AND MAN IN THE
NORTH COUNTRY

The Lord's Prayer and Bible readings were part of the daily morning ritual each schoolday, following the flag salute. Sometimes the passages the teacher chose were disturbing, like the day she read about how the world was to end in a fire of brimstone. Although she never explained the meaning of any verses she read, that day at recess Rose and Lily Barker led a Bible discussion. Their Aunt Ruby in Orford, New Hampshire, had heard a preacher make extremely graphic predictions about the end of time. We all listened, wide-eyed, and not only did it make for a worrisome day, but for weeks afterward I looked for signs of the upcoming apocalypse, though we never discussed it again.

Of the dozen and a half families in our neighborhood, only three ever went to church on Sunday morning. The Mac-Carthers seldom missed a Sunday service at the little Presbyterian church in the village; my family went there occasionally, too; and the Lapointes faithfully attended the Roman Catholic Church. All the others claimed to be "Home Baptists," and, although they never saw a minister at any other time, they invariably employed one for marriages and funerals.

Although most people in the neighborhood did not believe in church worship, they lived and fetched up their young 'uns according to very firm ideas of right and wrong. Proper morality and living codes had become firmly established in the North Country during the Victorian Age, and they lingered on and served us well during the discouraging Depression years.

One Biblical injunction taken seriously was the Fourth Commandment, "Six days thou shalt labor, and the seventh thou shalt rest." We all knew what constituted "work," and acceptable behavior on Sunday was rigidly defined. No one should work his team of horses on Sunday except to draw emergency feed or water for his stock. Pulling out a car that was stuck in the snow or the mud was questionable. One must not plant the garden, prune the orchard, boil maple syrup, spread manure, put on the double windows, clean the chimney, hoe the garden or harvest it (other than to pick a bit of lettuce for dinner), cut or split wood, or turn over the hay so it would dry faster.

However, if a cow were to slip through a hole in the barn floor on Sunday, naturally the Lord wouldn't want the meat wasted. It had to be shot and dressed off promptly. When an accident of that proportion happened, the farmer usually called in a few neighbors, supposedly to help, but actually to make it more "legal" and to share in the guilt.

A man could do all his regular chores, such as feeding and watering the animals and cleaning the cow stable, but he must not unload any hay or grain. He was allowed, however, to check the spring to determine whether it needed cleaning, to go into the maple woods to see if the sap was running, or to find out if the hay was dry in the back field.

His wife could not, with a clear conscience, wash cloths, scrub the floor, clean the windows, can vegetables, or make jelly. She could, however, spend hours cooking a huge Sunday dinner, as long as she did not fry doughnuts or bake bread, pies, or cakes intended for the upcoming week. She could not do any housecleaning, sewing, mending, or ironing unless the ironing was absolutely necessary in order for one to look presentable for a church service.

On Sunday, nearly every kind of amusement was ruled out, a directive inspired, no doubt, by our Puritan forefathers. Sports such as baseball, hunting, horseshoes, and even "toss" were forbidden, as were playing cards, croquet, checkers, or dominoes. Fishing and swimming were also deemed sinful, and dancing was not even considered. Although walking was allowed, horseback riding, unless you had to go somewhere in an emergency, was forbidden. That had a ring of pleasure about it. Shooting was not allowed, even if a fat woodchuck was devouring your garden. The neighbors would hear the shot.

It seemed to me that the only acceptable thing left to do on our day of rest was for everyone to watch everyone else very closely. If I were seen walking by the brook and it looked as if I might be fishing, or if I climbed onto the ridge pole of the barn to see the view, my mother would hear about it within a few hours.

There was a strong suspicion that retribution for the sins of the neighbors would be visited on one and all. Fear of punishment from on high kept the rules strictly observed, and everyone could quote instances of failure to comply. No one doubted the certainty of punishment, either in this world or the next. Aunt Myrtle warned, "Every stitch a woman sews on Sunday she will have to pull out with her nose in the hereafter." Climbing trees or hunting on Sunday was asking for trouble, either on the same day or shortly after. Fifty years earlier, John Clark's grandfather had drowned when his rowboat overturned on a sinful Sunday ride on the lake. Susie Long's baby was foolish and deformed, and everyone was certain it had been conceived on the Sabbath.

If by chance anyone slipped up, usually he or she felt it necessary to confess to someone promptly. An explanation and apology apparently made the sin less great, or at least made the transgressor feel better. Walter Gamble stopped my uncle when he was passing by the Gamble farm one spring to tell him about finding a bucket of maple sap, full and running over, when he checked his trees on Sunday morning. His Scottish blood couldn't bear the thought of the sap dripping on the ground for twenty-four hours, so he carefully took the full bucket off the tree and set it on the ground. He then went into the sugar house, got an empty bucket, and hung it up.

Monday morning, he found that his new bucket had filled with sap and the weight had pulled the spout out of the tree. It had fallen down and spilled both buckets. He wasn't surprised. He knew, deep in his bones, that he couldn't get away with doing that kind of thing on the Sabbath.

On rainy Sundays we were expected to read, write, or look at photo albums or postcards. My favorite activity was to study the stereopticon views with our ancient three-dimensional viewer. We had hundreds of pictures, ranging from New York skyscrapers ten stories tall to scenes from the western prairies. An old joke that was reprinted in the paper from time to time concerned a prospective employer hiring a new maid. "Do you have any religious views?" the man asked. "No, but I have some nifty photos of Niagara Falls," she replied. We had dozens of pictures of Niagara Falls, and dozens of the Holy Land.

Most of us youngsters resented the strict regimen on Sunday, especially since we had to work on Saturdays. When I was twelve, just to defy the "law," I climbed a few trees and took dips in Long Pond or our cool mountain brook. Roger Lincoln told me that he sometimes stuck his .22 Stevens rifle into his pant leg and walked stiff-legged until he and his dog were well out of sight of home. He never dared to shoot for fear of being heard, but he felt good anyway, knowing he was breaking one rule. David Finney used to sneak some *Captain Billy Whiz Bang, Police Gazette,* and *True Confessions* magazines to the barn on Sundays; there he read them safely out of sight in the hay barn. They'd been purloined from his older brothers and sisters, who had slid them under their mattresses.

These terrible deeds gave us all feelings of guilt. We might have enjoyed them more if we'd only been getting away with some rules set up by our parents, but our overdeveloped consciences had indeed learned "right" from "wrong." We never discussed our transgressions with anyone except the other boys and were especially careful that our tattling classmates, Rose and Lily, didn't overhear. It was bad enough that our guardian angel knew, without having all the neighbors in on it as well.

Oddly, when the Lapointes moved in from Canada with a new set of customs, the neighbors didn't panic. Their entire family dressed up faithfully every Sunday and went to the Roman Catholic mass, a custom that was, of course, acceptable. When they came home they still behaved properly according to the unwritten law of the community, and they had a big Sunday dinner. They then deviated from the rules and proceeded to have fun without trying to hide it. In their front yard, with crowds of relatives, they threw horseshoes and baseballs, sang, played guitars and accordions, and yelled loudly. Sometimes on a hot summer Sunday, if it looked like rain might come that evening, they actually spent the afternoon, after obtaining the priest's permission, putting hay into the barn.

Although such carryings-on dismayed the neighborhood judges, everyone was remarkably tolerant and tried to pretend it wasn't happening. After all, they came from "away," and they *were* different. I greatly envied the newcomers' freedom, though, and wished I'd come from "away," too.

At our home, Sunday was a quiet time meant for resting. Barn chores were necessary, but no other work was done, except for my mother's preparing a big Sunday dinner and cleaning up from it. We always put on our clean clothes to start the week, and Sunday morning was shaving time for the older boys and men in the family.

On rare occasions, people might shave on a weekday. A funeral, a family reunion, or a trip to the bank were all important enough to merit a clean shave, but ordinarily shaving was a once-a-week event. Beards were so rare they were stared at, and one had to be a Spanish-American War veteran to earn the right to wear one. Some elderly men wore moustaches, but they were not common, nor were sideburns. Although long facial hair was considered old-fashioned Civil War stuff, like tight breeches, a few day's stubble was acceptable.

Shaving was serious business, and we heard that the

wealthy men in town let their barbers do it. The men in our neighborhood bravely scraped their own faces each week with straight razors that had been laboriously and painstakingly sharpened on a long leather strap. Although safety razors were becoming popular, most frugal Yankees had no intention of buying a new blade or two each month.

I learned at an early age that it was never wise to talk to or in any other way distract one of my brothers while he was in the process of shaving, since everyone felt that his success depended on a minimum number of cuts. If I happened to be nearby when a slip of the razor occurred, I was likely to get the blame for it, guilty or not. Sunday morning was a good time to be out of the house.

Although we went to church rarely during the winter months, we attended more often in the seasons when the roads were good enough to go by car. To a country boy, the church service seemed mysterious. About the age of seven, I was very surprised when I first realized that the minister was actually saying something, not just making up a lot of words. I was equally amazed to learn that the mirror from which the organist could watch the congregation was actually just that. I had thought it was a tiny window on the organ from which the poor imprisoned woman was peering out at us lucky outsiders.

Since we weren't regular attendees, we had to make sure not to sit in a pew ordinarily occupied by a regular churchgoer. Seats were no longer bought and owned, as they once had been, but many families still hung on to the seat to which their ancestors had staked a claim and would scowl darkly at any stranger who got there first.

I didn't enjoy being boxed in by the straight-sitting women and black-suited men around me. The men, freshly shaven, usually had numerous scratches and nicks on their faces and sometimes sported blobs of soap in their ears. They wore black, highly polished shoes, black ties, and white shirts. All the women wore hats and gloves, and some wore shawls or capes. Everyone spoke in hushed whispers.

I was especially in awe of Duncan MacDonald, an elder who always sat in the third row. His family heritage in Scotland and Vermont had been so rugged that he was as hard as the rocks that covered his farm. Fearing nothing, he was willing to lecture the Almighty Himself when he thought He needed it. One morning he took over the service when the regular parson was absent. He prayed: "We've had quite enough rain already. In fact, we had enough a week ago. Now, let us have some sunshine, so we can get our hay dry." Another time, he said, "We have had far more than our share of all the troubles the human flesh is heir to. Show us better times, now, Lord."

Whether we went to church or not, we had a big Sunday dinner, and it seemed good not to eat the noon meal from a lunch pail. My mother always prepared good food, and since on Sundays we didn't work, there was no reason to hurry. Once in a great while, some relatives from out of town dropped in just before dinner without telling us they were coming. They knew for certain we'd be home. Ma never seemed to mind these surprises and always whipped up enough for everybody from the glass jars, meat crocks, and vegetable bins in the cellar. She considered the visits a welcome change and a challenge to her resourcefulness.

Sunday afternoons without company were boring, and I was often lonely. I became well acquainted with the brooks, woods, and little ponds around us and learned a lot about trees, plants, birds, and animals during those slow-moving days. By Monday I was usually eager to go back to school.

Whether or not the type of religion our neighborhood practiced had anything to do with it, we had almost no crime. All the same, a great deal of criminal activity was suspected, and we had an extremely thorough neighborhood watch. Every new family that moved in was observed carefully, and a detailed report on all their known activities was readied for all the neighbors. We were aware that John Barker had hired a variety of wild-looking men who drove noisy cars, drank large amounts of home brew, and hollered a lot. We never heard that any of them ever stole anything, but they were suspects every time a farmer mislaid a tool.

For many years Miz Tillson claimed that in August 1925 someone had stolen all the little cucumbers from her garden, but everyone suspected that she had simply forgotten to pick them when she should have, and they'd all grown into big ones. Mr. Finney stayed excited for several weeks one spring when he thought sneak thieves had stolen some of his maple syrup. His son David told me years later that his father had measured the syrup in the big steel drum when it was hot, and then again the next day, not realizing that it had contracted a great deal during the cooling-off process.

Since these minor happenings were all we had for excitement, we made the most of them, although they seemed pale compared with the florid murders, rapes, assaults, and robberies alleged to have happened a century earlier. I suspect that much of the talk about early crime was designed to scare any young potential criminals out of the idea.

One story I heard over and over concerned a man who once lived in our town who one day stole a pig from a neighbor. Because the neighbor had many pigs, the thief thought he probably wouldn't miss one of them. After a few months, however, he noticed that people were looking at him in a strange way and sometimes crossed the road to avoid talking to him.

Finally he became so concerned that he packed up his belongings and moved to Lowell, thirty miles away. Before three months had passed, he became aware that people were whispering that he had left his home town because he had stolen a sheep. So, a few weeks later he moved again. In his new residence, the same story circulated, but this time it concerned a cow he had swiped. A year later, in still another town, he was being pointed out as a former horse thief.

In desperation, he decided to move back to his home town. "At least there they know it was only a little pig," he told himself. When he returned, he was shocked to learn that the pig farmer had never missed the animal, and no one in town had suspected the theft.

Why this story was told so often I was unable to figure out, and I was never sure what the moral was. Possibly there were three:

1. Crime doesn't pay.
2. A body should always stay t' home where he belongs.
3. If a suitable rumor gets started, keep it going. It helps keep people honest.

Lying didn't go over very well in our neighborhood, and the rule most of the old-timers followed was to always tell one big enough so no one would believe it anyway. That made it perfectly acceptable.

Although swearing was common, both in school and out, it was done discreetly and never in front of the teacher or any older lady. Many men used a large variety of expressions that gave vent to their frustrations without actually taking the Lord's name in vain, although some of them came close. "Judas Priest," "Godfrey Mighty," "By Christmas," "I Snum," "Thunderation," "Drat," "Dang," and "By Gory" were common expressions, but when a situation demanded something stronger, even the elderly churchgoers easily found the right words.

One fall Fred Cheever bought a second-hand potato digger. Like most of the horse-and-buggy set, conversion to machinery did not sit easily with him. The digger happened to be a real lemon, however, and Calvin Jardine, who sold it to him, knew it. But Fred didn't complain and bravely worked with it, hoping somehow to get in his crop before winter.

One day Duncan MacDonald dropped by to say howdy while Fred, wrench in hand, was working on the contraption and swearing a blue streak. He looked up ashamedly when he saw Dunc. "You know," he said quietly, as he realized that the good Presbyterian elder had been taking in the situation for some time, "before I got this gol' 'rammed old wreck, I thought I had a pretty good chance of gettin' into Heaven. Now I know I ain't got no chance a'tall."

OF WORK AND WORRY

To a good Yankee, an idle body was considered a revolting sight. At school, "Get to work" was a common admonition if you gazed out the window on a winter day, hypnotized by the dark swirl of snowflakes coming directly toward you. "Get busy," Teacher said when you dreamily moved your pencil through space on a simulated Buck Rogers rocket trip to the newly discovered planet Pluto. "Is your arithmetic lesson done?" she asked if you suddenly smiled, remembering a funny joke you planned to tell a friend at recess. An idle mind was expected to spread the welcome mat for all sorts of temptation.

Our lives were lived by the Puritan work ethic. Hard work merited great respect and was the purpose for which humans had been placed on this earth. It exemplified whatever was good, honest, and noble and was the means by which we could be a credit to our family, ancestors, and country. Eventually hard work would even earn us a spot in Paradise. Some of the most frequently sung hymns were "Come Labor On," "Christian Work for Jesus," "Bringing in the Sheaves," and, of course, "Work for the Night is Coming."

Relaxation and fun, we were made to understand at an early age, although not completely evil, came mighty close. A body was always made to feel guilty about relaxing unless everyone else was resting as well, which was a rare occurrence in our neighborhood, except on Sunday. Playing was even more suspect. On a Sunday it was sinful, and on a weekday it interfered with good, honest work. Many pious elders thought that play was a clever device invented by Satan to lead the unwary into far worse things and should be handled sparingly and with great care. In short, we'd better be prepared to explain and apologize if we were having too much fun anytime.

Although no season was actually restful on the farm, fall was especially frantic. In school we read that the Indians held corn festivals, and the Italians, grape festivals, but we Yankees were far too busy harvesting and storing to stop for nonsense like dancing and carousing. My brothers, sisters, and I had been reared on Aesop's fable of the industrious ant and the foolish, frolicking grasshopper. According to this much-quoted tale, the fun-loving grasshopper opted to spend his summer and fall days cavorting and making merry. While his neighbor, the noble, busy ant, worked day and night storing food for winter, the hopper sang, danced, played his fiddle, and set a sorry example for insects and humans alike. Come winter, according to Aesop, the ant lived high on the hog until spring. The grasshopper, however, who hadn't even mended his roof, froze, starved, and met a humiliating, miserable demise.

So we, like the ant, in order to ensure that we would stay warm and well fed, each fall picked, dug, toted, shelled, husked, split, and piled. All over the neighborhood the women pickled, canned, dried, jellied, juiced, and jammed, since Grammy Corkins had predicted, just as she had for six decades, "the worst winter we've had in fifty years."

Because of our pessimism, we always stored far too much food when we were getting ready for winter. Even the rats and mice that infiltrated the stone-lined barns and cellars could not handle the surplus. There was always plenty left over in the spring, even if a hard-up relative or friend had experienced hard sleddin' and needed extra produce. At the end of each winter, however, it seemed to me that we took tons of unused potatoes, apples, turnips, beets, carrots, cabbage, and onions out of the cellar and dumped them or fed them to the pigs. Each spring we vowed to grow less, but if there were 200 seeds in an envelope, we planted each one. Since they all grew, we harvested the results, hauled the produce to the cellar, and stored it, knowing full well that, come next spring, once more we would carry most of it outdoors again.

In the midst of a winter blizzard, however, when we went downstairs to our cellar and brought up a pan of firm, hard potatoes, a squash, a jar of creamy corn, and a bowl of apples, or when we took a lantern upstairs to the attic for some butternuts and popcorn, our labors in the fall seemed worthwhile. Enjoying our bounty next to a roaring wood fire, I appreciated my family's industrious, albeit pessimistic, nature. But each spring when I helped haul the unused harvest back up the cellar stairs, I wondered if Aesop's hard-working ant was having the same problem. Maybe he, too, was secretly wishing he had taken off a few days of the previous summer and gone to a party with the grasshopper.

During autumn in northern Vermont, the days were brilliantly clear and cool, and the crisp, cold nights invigorating. Geese and other birds flew south in large flocks, squirrels dashed to and fro, and the air was full of the delicious smell of leaves and earth. Most people were only dimly aware of these happenings, however, because they were working so hard to get ready for winter. All the daylight hours we were not in school, we were expected to help bring in the harvest and firewood, bank the house, and put on the storm windows. The heifers had to be rounded up, driven in from the back pasture, and, very much against their will, tied up in the barn.

A good harvest was not only a necessity for survival but also a trophy of success. Men sometimes stopped total strangers who were passing by their farms and invited them to inspect their well-stuffed barns, silos, and woodsheds. Anyone who stored barely enough to squeak through the winter was branded as a "lazy, good-for-nothing, ne'er-do-well" who could plan on being talked about when the folks with better judgment got together.

A bulging barn was far more likely to merit respect than

a new Buick, and a wife with a well-filled pantry gained more admiration than one who sported a well-filled bathing suit. In fact, whenever a man "took unto hisself a wife," no one asked whether she was a "neat looker," or if she was likely to be a good mother. They never expressed any interest whatsoever in whether she could read or write well, play the piano at Grange, or sing in the choir. That could wait. The big concern was whether "the lad has gotten hisself a good worker," and whether "she'll be able to turn out a passin' mess o' vittles, and to wash, sew, and mend, and help out properly in the barn and field." Although our neighbors were strait-laced, a woman with a few shady happenings in her past was far more acceptable to the local critics than a lazy lay-abed who wasted valuable time putting on makeup and reading magazines.

Although one's work habits seemed to be very important, reputation was the real concern. It didn't seem to matter so much whether a person actually was accomplishing anything but whether he or she *seemed* to be working hard. Only one small deviation from the "rules" could cause a reputation to be shattered forever. I never heard Louise Forge described in anything but scornful terms, and only because of an event that had taken place years before I was born, when she was first married. Joe Waugh had wandered into the Forges' sugar house, obviously lolligagging himself when he should have been t' home a-workin'. There he found Lou combing her hair in front of a tiny mirror as she boiled sap, acting not at all ashamed of herself. He never forgot the incident, nor did he let anyone else.

Susie Day's reputation, too, was in tatters and would never be fully redeemed, even though she had performed a lifetime of good works. One day a curious neighbor spotted a *True Story* and several pulpy movie magazines on her kitchen table, under the Sears Roebuck catalogue. "They say she reads a lot of sinful papers instead of doing mending and fancy work," someone would always comment when her name came up in conversation. Ella Robbins was rumored to steal a few minutes from her cooking and washing to write poetry now and then, and this made her somewhat questionable, too.

Once a reputation was acquired, it could never be lived down. We all knew that if a girl began to wear makeup at an early age, or a boy bought a car before he was twenty-one, neither could probably ever again be completely trusted, even though she might later become president of the Ladies' Aid, and he chairman of the Board of Selectmen. Both they and their wayward parents would be regarded suspiciously until the day we read their obituaries in the *Hardwick Gazette*.

Because judgment was passed more on a person's labors than his or her accomplishments, it was considered far more important to look constantly busy than to actually get anything done, or to get it done quickly. The woodpile was an example. Often, wood was drawn from wherever it had been sawed, and then piled carefully in the front yard, so the neighbors could see it for a few weeks. Later it was hauled to the back yard and once again piled nearer the woodshed. Finally it was moved inside and piled again.

One year Steely Lincoln was bringing wood in from the sugar house and piling it in the yard. In the midst of unloading the wagon, he went into the kitchen for a drink of water. When he returned to his work, he absentmindedly forgot where he was and started to throw the wood back into the wagon. His puzzled wife came out of the kitchen and straightened him out before he got the wagon quite full, but Steely, embarrassed, felt he ought to confess to the neighbors. None of them seemed to think it too odd, however. The main thing was to keep busy.

At school, as soon as we were big enough, we were expected to take our turns at the chores—filling the woodbox, shoveling the path in winter, sweeping the floor, going after the water, and agitating the chemical toilets. We didn't object, because we knew those things had to be done, and we'd been brought up to help. The "idle hands are the devil's workshop" philosophy kept the roadsides trimmed, pastures cleared, carrots thinned, fences mended, and hand raking done around stones; and it prevented a lot of juvenile delinquency—but it left precious little time for swimming, fishing, looking at clouds, hunting woodchucks, and flying kites.

The programs at community events were often organized around the subject of work. We read in the county paper of the Farm Bureau or church youth having public debates, and one favorite topic dealt with the merits of city life versus country life. Those who championed country living stressed the fresh air, the variety of work on a farm as opposed to that of a dull, tedious factory job, and the wonderful advantages of growing one's own food. The opponents favored the city life that offered long, work-free weekends, week-long vacations, and a short fifty-hour work week. Those on the side of living in the country always won the debate, since the judges were elderly farmers. They and most other rural adults saw nothing that wasn't right with wholesome, healthy fourteen-hour work days.

The work habit was so firmly ingrained in most people's lives that retirement was not easy. After seven decades of hard work, a man or woman often found it impossible to slow down without feeling extremely guilty. My grandmother, after her family had left home and she lived completely alone, still baked a half dozen apple pies at a time. "Can't let all those apples go to waste," she'd say. She found it equally difficult not to fry a large pan of doughnuts and bake a big batch of bread every few days, even though there was no longer anyone at home to eat the results of her labors.

One of my uncles, at the age of eighty, moved into a house in the village with little to care for except a small garden. He, and many retirees like him, continued to get up faithfully every morning at 5:00, however, just as he had when it was his job to farm 200 acres.

Even if a man wanted to slow down, sometimes the neighbors wouldn't let him. Some years before I was born, when Zed Hollis became seventy-five, he announced he'd had plumb enough of cows and haying. He sold his farm and moved into town, vowing he had earned the right to take life easy and, "by crotch, I'm a-goin' to do it." He hadn't reckoned with his retired neighbors, who felt he shouldn't set a bad example the first day he was there.

"Do you know what old man Hollis did his first day in town?" one of them disgustedly asked my father the next week. "He didn't do a damn thing. He took and set right on his front veranda where the whole town could see him in a gol' 'ram rocking chair, and the old fool never stirred a bone from noon 'til supper."

"Are you positive?" my father asked. "How do you know?"

"How do I know?" the man began to shout. "My God, man, why, I live right across the street from him. I sat right on my own piazza all afternoon and, by gory, I watched him."

Most farmers never retired at all. They stayed around to help their sons or the new owner and "died in the harness" whenever possible.

For years the model for human behavior in our neighborhood was prim and proper, fretful and hard-working Miz Tootson. Tilly was reputed to be so industrious, so efficient, and such an early riser that she invariably had the lamps filled, the jugs emptied, the beds made, and the breakfast dishes done before the rest of the family was out of bed. Most of the time, though, such illustrations were deadly serious. Work and worry shaped our lives, and our seniors never ran out of proverbs and examples to prove their value.

Worry was held in nearly as much esteem as hard work. "Only a fool don't worry," I often heard one of the old men say, and, like most of our neighbors, he was a professional. The list of things to fret over was endless: money, health, weather, taxes, roads, children, crops, cows, horses, a trip to town, the buildings, and on and on. When there was extra time, it was spent listening in on the phone so one could worry about the neighbors' troubles, as well.

Everything about the forthcoming winter was worth extra concern, and it was fashionable to profess not to be able to enjoy summer and fall because of it. Will the water pipes freeze? Will rats eat the oats? Will the chimney catch fire? Will the wood hold out? Will the heavy snow break down the barn roof? Any Yankee worth his mince pie for breakfast could worry almost full time about the winter, and an extra-good Vermonter even worried a bit about the winter after next.

GENERATION GAP

If youth and a youthful outlook were at all admired in our neighborhood during my school years, no young person was aware of it. Mothers might coo over one another's babies, but all adults regarded older children with suspicion, at least until they reached voting age. Many oldsters we knew always referred to anyone under age twelve as a "little stink," "little snot," or "brat." Those in their early teens were called "young hoodlums" or "rowdies," no matter how exemplary their behavior might be.

Veneration was expected not only by our teachers and family members but also by any old bum who wandered by. Naturally we greatly resented that so much power seemed to rest with the older generation, but since everyone was conditioned from babyhood to respect one's elders, discipline was seldom a problem at home or in school. My family felt, as did most of the neighbors, that the only proper way to fetch up a child was to keep him "in his place." If any young 'un tried to express an opinion in front of a group of adults, he was immediately shushed or pointedly ignored while the parents of the wayward youth looked properly ashamed at their failure in child rearing.

We were taught to equate age with wisdom. If a man under twenty-one tried to buy a car, a cow, or a farm on his own, without having an older person with him, the seller was somewhat wary of making the transaction. A youth was expected to take along his father, an older brother, or a willing neighbor to guide him on any business deal, even if he was only opening a bank account or buying a suit of clothes. Young mothers invariably took an older woman with them when they went shopping for baby clothing or household goods.

Many parents encouraged their children to be dependent on them for as long as possible; teaching them to be afraid and suspicious was one method they used to keep them on the farm. It was always difficult to be friends with any of the Williams boys—their parents worked hard at keeping them mad at everyone so that they could have a strong family clan and an abundance of cheap labor. Few youths in my school were encouraged to rise to greater heights than those of their daddy.

Another method by which adults kept firm control was to keep a tight rein on the purse strings. They managed every bit of the meager amount of money that circulated in the area, and no child received an allowance. We might get a nickel occasionally, but usually only if we could prove we really needed it for a worthwhile purpose, such as a school picture.

No one was paid for work at home, even when we became teenagers, and if I or my friends worked a few days for a neighbor, we almost never received any pay for that, either. The neighbor usually paid back the favor in some kind of work swap with our family, or in goods. If money was involved, the employer would "settle up" with our parents, but never with us. The consensus was that teens did not need any money and were too immature to handle it anyway.

Almost no young adult was paid according to what he was worth on the economic scale. "How little will he or she work for?" was the primary discussion when hiring a new teacher, minister, store clerk, or sawmill hand. Farm laborers, woodsworkers, and those who worked on the roads were also far underpaid. Often young men worked eighty-hour weeks at very difficult tasks for only their board and a tiny amount of cash. Most had been conditioned to believe that hard outdoor work was more manly, and therefore more acceptable to their peers, than a better-paying position in a shop or as a salesman. Young people were also expected to work in all kinds of weather and to work twice as hard as their elders. When farmers needed a great deal of extra help, many of them made a practice of hiring a semi-stupid, extra-strong braggart like Guy Storey to work with the rest of the gang in the hope of pushing the less rugged lads to greater output. Raises were granted not as a result of job proficiency or additional skill but only because of a need, such as getting married, having a new child, or buying a home.

One result of the prevailing attitude of adult superiority was an enormous communication gap. We learned to keep our dreams and opinions mostly to ourselves. By the time I was in the seventh grade, for example, Roger Lincoln and I had learned that it was best not to tell any grown-up of our exciting plans for Sunday afternoon. It usually worked out much better if they found out what we'd done no earlier than Sunday evening when we returned after exploring another part of the mysterious back country that was reputed to be so terrifying. We found, contrary to what I'd been told, that there really was not any quicksand at Mud Pond, and that kidnapping gypsies, boy-eating bears, bobcats, and panthers posed no threat in the deep woods. We discovered that dropoffs didn't suddenly grab people who were innocently swimming, and that guns, fireworks, and bonfires could be handled safely before one reached retirement age.

Aaron Jillson sadly learned the wisdom of withholding any future plans from his parents the Sunday he announced that he was going to the lake for the first time. His father's response was immediate. "I don't want you going near any confounded water," he told Aaron firmly, "until you learn how to swim."

A TRIP TO TOWN

At least once each winter I went to town on Saturday with one of my brothers. When I was in the early grades, I went as a passenger on the team-drawn sled, but later I went to help load grain or fertilizer at the feed store or to get sawdust from the sawmill for bedding the cattle.

Winter was a good time to look over the town, because we could stay longer than on summer days, when we had to hurry back to do the haying. In winter our only deadline was to be home in time to do the evening chores. Although it was unhurried, the trip was seldom comfortable because the temperature was likely to be below zero with the wind blowing. I looked forward to every stop, not only to enjoy the unfamiliar sights and smells but also to get warm.

"The Bend," our trading center, was so named because the railroad had been built through town in a big loop. The railroad station, the town's hub, was surrounded by a water tower, a freight office, a creamery, and a large coal station. On the main street were also five stores, a post office, a church, a grammar school, a large sawmill, a boarding house, a dance hall, a pool room, a feed store, a barbershop, a blacksmith shop, and a garage.

Surrounding the village were thousands of acres of wooded mountains, and the stores served numerous families who lived on little farms and homesteads tucked into clearings in the forest. Many of them came to town on Saturdays to shop, as we did, and to swap their home-produced eggs, butter, maple syrup, firewood, and sometimes a side of beef for coffee, tobacco, flour, oatmeal, and kerosene. Most families had lived in the area for generations, so everyone knew one another and lingered for a visit. Although a few farmers took their milk to town each day and bought an item or two each time, as an excuse to go into the stores, most, like us, had our milk picked up by truck and went to town only once or twice each month.

One winter day when I was eleven, we started for town about nine o'clock, after morning chores were finished. Ned and Pat, our two big black work horses, were harnessed and hitched to the two-piece sled. The crated six dozen eggs we were taking to the store were carefully covered with two horse blankets to keep them from freezing. We were bundled up in heavy sheepskin coats, mittens, scarfs, and touques, and I crawled under the blankets to keep warm. The six-mile ride was mostly downhill, and the horses trotted occasionally, so the ride took only an hour and a half.

As our sled approached the Bend we could see a misty cloud of smoke floating over the buildings that clustered in the valley. The coal-burning locomotives, milk plant, and sawmill poured thick clouds of smoke and steam into the sky, and smoke from dozens of wood-burning stoves and furnaces billowed from chimneys and drifted hazily over the town, trapped there by the cold, icy downdrafts from the hills on each side.

Compared with our quiet farm, the village was very noisy. In the morning the noisiest place was the milk plant, where dozens of trucks and teams unloaded their ten-gallon metal jugs of milk. After being weighed, the milk was loaded on refrigerated tank cars and shipped by train to Boston. The little railroad was nicknamed the "Sour Milk Limited" because so many carloads of milk left the area each day.

Our horses were extremely nervous among all the unfamiliar cars, trains, and people, and we had to be ready to grab them quickly whenever a puffing locomotive tooted its loud whistle or the sawmill blew off steam.

It felt good to get out of the cold sled, hitch the sweaty

horses to a hitching post, cover them with blankets, and dash into the warm general store, where the pleasant scent of oranges, peanuts, bread, soap powder, and apples filled the air. Since I wasn't buying anything, I was free to wander around and look at the large bunches of bananas hanging from the ceiling, the glass jars filled with hard candy, the chocolate bars, soda water, and other costly items. My brother bought a bag of store cookies for our lunch, and I was allowed to fill the bag with the various kinds of cookies displayed in the tantalizing open boxes.

Many other items were sold in bulk, such as tripe, cheese, pickles, crackers, peanut butter, dates, nuts, and salt pork. They were in boxes, barrels, or tubs, so we could look everything over before the clerk weighed and wrapped it. In addition to the food, in the back of the store were racks and boxes of new-smelling clothing, heaps of footwear, tools, and even a kerosene pump.

No one browsed through the store and picked out what he wanted, however. We gave our list to the clerk or read it to him, and he got everything for us. He used a long-handled set of grippers to reach cans and packages from the high shelves, and he often brought out a variety of different brands for his customers to select from. Everyone waiting knew what the folks ahead of them were buying, their clothing sizes, and how much they paid for everything. The clerk made out a slip for everyone and added up the amount by hand. Some people had their groceries "charged," and these he listed on a white pad with a carbon and yellow second sheet. Shopping was not a speedy business.

As I waited, I continued to wander through the store, listening to the group of men who were sitting near the warm floor register discussing the news as they smoked their pipes. I watched two men silently play checkers and was fascinated by the big brass spittoon. In spite of the sign hanging over it that said, "We Aim to Please, Will You Aim, Too, Please?" there was evidence all around of the tobacco chewers' misdirected shots.

Everyone looked up when bewhiskered Mike MacDonald, who lived high on Walden Mountain, walked in the door. He had hiked five miles from his home to the village, wearing a knapsack and carrying the snowshoes he had used for the first three miles. Mike always came to the store in November and loaded up his truck with several barrels of flour, cornmeal, two or three bags of sugar that weighed 100 pounds each, two five-gallon cans of kerosene, and tins of coffee, tea, and other staples to feed his large family all winter. After it began to snow and he had no road, he walked out only occasionally to get a few perishables that he could easily carry, like compressed yeast cakes.

Mike, like everyone else in the store, was in no hurry and talked with everyone. Loitering was not only permitted in all the stores, it was encouraged. The proprietor of any business that served the farmers felt that when a man had come several miles to shop, he was entitled to "set a spell."

When we'd sold our eggs and bought all the groceries on Ma's list, we put them into the wooden box on the sled and went next door to the hardware store to get some nails and harness parts for winter repairs. The store smelled of leather, oils, and hot soldering. Although we didn't stop there long, while I waited for my brother to buy his items I had a chance to look over the sugar equipment, milking machines, churns, kerosene lamps, farm tools, guns, traps, gardening equipment, and wood-cutting supplies.

Our next stop was the barber shop, since my brother said he would either have to get a haircut or stay out of the woods during hunting season. The shop was a tiny house that had been made over, and it had a red-and-white-striped pole in front. As we walked in, a strong scent of shaving cream, bay rum, and other hair tonics filled the air. There was an old church pew to sit on, some beat-up magazines, and a punchboard for anyone wanting to take a chance on winning a prize. Since many men waited until spring to get a haircut, nobody else was in the shop. Time passed quickly because I had never before seen a *Police Gazette,* with its scantily clad ladies.

The feed store, where we stopped next, distributed nearly as much news as it did fertilizer, and, as usual, several retired farmers were hanging out there when we arrived. The fragrances of beet pulp, bran, cottonseed meal, fertilizer, and burlap hung heavily in the air.

The topic of conversation that day was the baby scandal. Earlier in the month the Grange had given away a baby pig at one of its card parties and had made a grand affair of it. The piglet was dressed up in a bonnet, put in a baby basket, and furnished with a nurse and bottle.

Only a portion of that story reached the back country, however. We got our information from Mrs. Forge, who had called everyone she could think of to report that the sinful Grange was raffling off babies. A day or two later we heard from another source that it was a baby someone had found on the village dump. "Probably," Mrs. Coomer surmised, "a kid that had been abandoned by one of those horrid high school girls."

Even though the truth of the baby raffle had since become widely known, it was the only big news around, so everyone kept it going. As we loaded the bags of grain, we also picked up such lesser items as who had run out of water, and whose dairy herd had the scours. Going to town was a good way to keep up with the bad news we'd missed on the telephone.

The trip home, with our heavy load of grain, was slow, because the horses stopped frequently going up the long, steep hills. We walked most of the way, not only to lighten the load for the team but also to keep warm.

Although it was an exciting change to visit town and see the people, trains, and stores, it felt good to be back home, and I nuzzled close to the hot cookstove as we drank the mugs of hot cocoa Ma had waiting for us. Already it was getting dusky, and I still had to help unload the sled, feed the chickens, pick up their eggs, and dump out their drinking water before it got dark and everything froze up for the night. The trip had taken nearly all day.

WASTE NOT, WANT NOT

Waste not, want not, is a maxim I would teach,
Let your watchword be dispatch, and practice what you preach.
Do not let your chances, like sunbeams pass you by,
For you'll never miss the water, 'til the well runs dry.
                    —popular song by Rowland Howard

Proverbs relating to thrift were nearly as popular in School District No. 9 as those that had to do with hard work. Waste was considered a cardinal sin, as bad as lust and avarice. Not a bit of paper was thrown away until it had been thoroughly covered on both sides. Paper used on only one side was put into the scratch paper drawer and used later for figuring arithmetic problems or for practicing writing. A plain, unpainted pencil with no eraser was expected to last a minimum of one month, so we tried not to break the point too often. A fat rubber eraser was supposed to last all year, and books, nearly forever.

Water was another valuable commodity, since we had to carry it each day from the Tylers' farmhouse. If any remained in the cup we'd been drinking from, it was dumped into a washbasin and used later for washing our hands. One pail of water minus the amount sloshed over us enroute from the Tylers' to school was expected to last all day.

At home, as at school, water was carefully conserved, and hot water was considered precious, even though it was "het" with wood. If the kettle of water on the stove was hot, an enterprising housewife would scrub a floor, a ceiling, or a child. "No need to just let it bile away."

Douglas Anderson, who lived in the village, was asked to keep an eye on the parsonage one cold winter night when the Presbyterian preacher and his wife had been called out of town. While he was filling the stoves with wood, he noticed that the water tank connected to the kitchen stove was full of mighty hot water.

His Scotch blood began to thicken, so he promptly filled up the bathtub and took the first tub bath of his life. After he had dressed and was leaving, he noticed that the tank was getting well heated up again. So he went home and fetched his wife, Agnes, and she had her first tub bath, too. Naturally, nobody would have known anything about the episode, except for the fact that Doug, proud of his resourcefulness, told everyone.

There was no visible class distinction between the "haves" and the "have nots" in our school, because everyone was a "have not." We all dressed more or less alike. Everybody's family owned a second-hand Ford, Chevrolet, or Plymouth that probably cost between $25 and $200. No one had electricity, and for most, indoor plumbing was a luxury that had not yet arrived. Even the toilet paper at school was a novelty, since catalogues and newspapers were the rule in our privies at home.

Most houses in the back country were in great need of paint, and very few barns and sheds had ever been painted. Still, ours was not a tumbledown neighborhood. Nearly everyone kept the buildings sound, the roofs patched, and fences in good repair. Hard work accomplished much of what there was no money to buy, and because we raised most of our own food, none of us starved. Still, I think my family fully expected to see the wolf on the front steps every morning when they opened the door.

Since the government didn't subsidize poverty, our town, like most, had an Overseer of the Poor who helped out destitute widows, the crippled, blind, and simple-minded. Mr. Keith bought groceries and other necessities and occasionally paid Mrs. Harvey twenty-five cents to feed a tramp. All the recipients' names were published in the town report each year, with the amount they received, so no able-bodied citizen ever applied for help, except in desperate circumstances.

Most people in our neighborhood weathered the Depression rather well. Survival skills passed down from pioneer grandparents and a passion for thrift gave them a great advantage over the unemployed workers in the cities.

"Waste not, want not" was not only a slogan and a song, it was also our way of life. We were not to throw away clothes or any other worldly goods for which we or someone else might ever have a possible use. Homemade clothes, which almost never fit, were handed down in each family from child to child. When there were no more children in the family to wear them, any garment still remotely wearable was passed on to a neighbor or relative, with no apology on the part of the giver or receiver.

The winter I was in sixth grade I had to wear a thick pair of wool pants that had probably been sewn before the Civil War, because they looked like the tight-legged style Abraham Lincoln had worn at his inauguration. Since most everyone else was wearing wide-legged pants, I was a bit ashamed of the way I looked. Still, they were better than the knickers and long stockings I had been wearing previously.

One day near the end of the winter, though, time caught up with my breeches, and they disintegrated when I caught them on the chalk tray while I was doing arithmetic problems at the blackboard. Luckily, I had on long underwear, but I was very embarrassed, nevertheless, and took a lot of ribbing from my schoolmates. That night Ma, in her big box of passed-down clothing, found another pair of pants that were not quite as old and not more than a couple of sizes too big. My ripped pants were cut into long strips to be braided into rugs.

Everybody wore clothes not only long after they had faded, but also after they'd been patched and repatched and sometimes dyed. Suits were turned inside out when the outsides got too shiny. Every housewife spent her evenings and every other spare moment mending, darning socks, turning worn collars and cuffs, repairing holes in sweaters, and sewing patches on garments that were coming apart. New clothes were so uncommon that Judah MacDougal always left the big paper labels on his overalls until they were washed so that everyone would notice they were new.

Food was never wasted, either, and leftovers from the dinner at noon usually constituted the main part of that evening's supper. We always had plenty of hash, soups, and puddings that my mother concocted from leftovers, and there was still plenty for Peggy, our collie dog, and our several cats. The pigs were given all our apple and potato parings, and the chickens got any moldy bread.

Most families carried their thrift to great extremes and often deposited quantities of dilapidated items in their sheds and lofts, hoping that someone would find a use for them. Our shed chamber, as the attic was called, contained large boxes of completely worn-out shoes and mismatched gloves full of holes. Several barrels of dry corncobs stood in one corner to be used for smoking meat, although we might use only eight or ten cobs each year. Neatly stacked were boxes of hopelessly rusted nails, rotten leather harness straps, broken window glass, and many pieces of heavy string and rope that were too short or too far gone for any possible use.

Also in the shed chamber, hanging on a nail, was a large rag bag in which were collected clothes no longer good enough for washing windows or making rugs. These were sold for five or ten cents a bag to the peddler who came by once a year, and he, in turn, sold them to salvage companies to be used for making paper. We also religiously saved stiff old paint brushes, broken bottles, rusty tin cans, broken shoelaces, and worn-out rubber boots, for what reason I never figured out, since even the ragman didn't want them. Rummaging through the attic was one of my favorite pastimes as a boy, though, and I spent many happy hours there on rainy days.

Once I visited the children of our friends the Findlays. Their ancestors, who were more recently arrived from a hard life in the British Isles than mine, had found it even more impossible to discard anything. Each room in their enormous house was like an attic—filled with catalogues, magazines, and newspapers collected over many years, bundles of peacock feathers, old guns, bottles, quarantine signs, swords and medals from the Civil War, powder kegs and horns, cowboy spurs, bear traps, an old loom, a flax wheel, candle molds, homemade tools, and much more. It was a boy's paradise.

Just as it was considered sinful to throw away anything without a good reason, likewise one was not expected to buy anything new unless he could prove to himself and his neighbors that he really needed it. Froth Hudson bought his wife, Gracie, a newfangled gasoline-powered washing machine in 1932, the year I was in the fourth grade. The neighborhood was aghast. "Gol' 'ram fool oughta have a guardian," was the common description of his folly.

"Eat it up, wear it out, make it do, or go without" was the code of the Hills, and also of the Cheevers, the Andersons, the Lincolns, and just about everybody else.

Time was another commodity we must not waste, and everyone had great respect for it. Being on time was as important as being frugal. To be late not only brought disgrace upon yourself and your family, but it also was considered a sin comparable to being lazy or playing pool on Sunday.

A clock was often a family's most expensive possession, and it governed everyone's life. In my great-grandfather's account book, one item indicates that he paid $24 for a clock in the very early 1800s. In a time when a gallon of whiskey or a pair of shoes went for 60 cents, a casket cost $2.50, and a new house complete with cellar, two chimneys, hardwood floors, windows, and plastered walls could be built for $350, $24 was a tremendous amount.

It seems odd that the people in my neighborhood, since they had no trains to catch and no time clocks to worry about, should have had such an acute sense of time, but they did. Breakfast was always on my family's table at eight, after morning chores were done. Dinner was at noon, and that didn't mean five minutes before or five minutes past. It didn't mean when the vittles were done, either, or when someone got back from the store. Supper was at five, and as with all meals, unless there was a real emergency, both the meal and the folks eating it were expected to be ready.

Most people I knew didn't go anywhere often, but when they did, they planned to be early. As a teenager, I was embarrassed and uncomfortable when my family showed up a half hour early for a funeral, but we usually found several other neighbors already waiting. We arrived at my sister's high school graduation before the janitor had opened the building.

"If you can't be there on time, better not bother to go at all" and "Better early than late" were phrases I heard often at home and at school. Latecomers were stared at, commented on, and would have had to be stone deaf not to know they were being pointed out as bad examples of humanity.

It was expected that all neighborhood bees would start on time. When Snort Finney started up his wood-sawing rig at 8:30 in the morning, he expected the neighborhood men to have done their barn chores, have "et" their breakfast, have laced up their boots, and be ready to saw wood.

Sometimes a little help was necessary to meet the deadlines. "I came into the house a little early one day," Herman Barker told us at school, "and my mother was setting the clock back because she didn't have dinner quite ready. She made me promise not to tell, and my father thought he had set his watch wrong."

Every man valued his pocket watch, and some older folks had very elaborate ones. An expensive fat gold watch in the vest pocket of one's dress-up clothes, with a gold chain stretching across the front, was a badge of success. Many watches had fancy engraving on the back, and some had covers that had to be flicked open before you could see the face. Most men, and a few boys, had pocket watches that had cost a dollar or less. If they weren't dropped on the floor, they would keep good time for years.

Although nearly everyone was obsessed with being on time, people often lost track of the days of the week. Every home had two or three calendars in each room, but that didn't always help. Few homes had radios until the late 1930s, and no one saw a daily paper. If a family didn't have children in school, each day was pretty much like the day before, so no one seemed terribly surprised when folks showed up for some event a day or two early or late.

One winter Sunday some years before I was born, my family was on the way to church in the sleigh when they overtook Duncan MacDonald headed for town with his team of horses and a big load of logs on a double sled. Since Duncan was a church elder and, unlike my family, attended faithfully, they were shocked to see him working on the Sabbath. He was equally surprised when he turned around and noticed them. "Where are you folks going all dressed up?" he called as he pulled over his rig. "To church," they answered.

"Church! Why, today ain't Sunday." Then he turned pale. "By gravy, it is." Turning the large load of logs around in the narrow road wasn't easy, but he managed it. "I've got to get home and stop Hanna," he yelled back. "She's just starting to make pies."

Dunc and Hanna were quite late for church that day, but they sat in their usual pew, and there was no hint, either in their expressions or conversation, that anything unusual had happened along the way.

TOWN MEETING

The year I was in the seventh grade, the town school board decided that the children in their country schools should have the same opportunity as those in the village to examine government in action. So, on Town Meeting Day we were excused from school to attend the big event with our families.

I had often heard that the first Tuesday in March was the worst possible time to have a town meeting. In Salem, where they thought up the idea, spring had already arrived, but in northern Vermont, it was still winter and a critical time for a chronic cold-climate disease called cabin fever. More than at any other time of year, tempers were frayed and nerves were wearing thin. No one seemed to be doing anything worth talking about, travel was difficult, and there hadn't been a good rumor circulated for weeks.

Cabin fever made the people in our neighborhood scrutinize the listing of upcoming town business word for word, to see what high-falutin' ideas the village folk had thought up that they wanted the poor, hard-working farmers to help pay for. Everyone studied the newly printed reports item by item to see if any town official might possibly have squandered a few dollars during the year. Throughout the winter, before I went to my first town meeting, I heard the local men grumble bitterly about the selectmen, who always had their own roads fixed up first, and the village school directors, who "didn't care nothing about the one-room schools in the back country." "Come March meetin', them folks are going to be put in their proper place, by thunder." I was braced for lots of action.

149

The big day arrived, and with dozens of other people, Roger Lincoln, Helen Jillson, and I climbed the three flights of stairs to the town hall. I was surprised at the big crowd, and especially to see so many children there. Everywhere, people were gathering in little groups and chatting as they waited for the moderator to gavel the meeting to order. Since no one paid any attention to an eleven-year-old, I wandered from group to group, taking notes for the Walter Winchell–type report I planned to make at school the next day. Several library trustees were plotting how to best plead their case to get more money for books. The three school directors were scheming over the best strategy to introduce their ideas of closing two more rural schools and converting the village school's heating system from wood to coal. The road commissioner and selectmen were in a huddle trying to decide whether they should try to raise some extra money to spread gravel over a few more miles of road or allow the farmers to continue to live with mud and low taxes.

Most of the farmers were discussing milk, cows, and feed supplies, and a large number of them apparently hadn't seen one another since the last March meeting. I overheard two village men as they pointed out one of the farmers. They howled in laughter because, one of them told the other, the week before he'd bought a pair of newfangled zipper overshoes, and after he'd worn them home he couldn't figure out how to work the zipper. He'd had to sleep with them on that night and return to the store for assistance the next day.

At exactly ten o'clock Jesse Wilcox, a wiry farmer from the other side of town, stood up on the stage. He peered down at the crowd, looking us all over as if he were searching for someone, and then began to hit the stand in front of him with a wooden hammer. He clenched his "boughten" teeth a lot and wore a very old suit coat with wide lapels, black tie, and baggy pants that came barely to the top of his worn but polished high black shoes. It took several bangs of his wooden hammer before everybody sat down and was quiet, in spite of the fact that he was obviously a greatly respected town official.

It was the first time I'd attended an organized meeting, and it was not run at all the way I'd thought it would be. The moderator believed in wasting neither time nor money, and he encouraged no discussion. I had heard, at our sawing bee that winter, that "the gol' 'ram fool up front does just exactly what the selectmen and the Grange tell him to." As the day progressed, though, I could see that nobody ever told him to do anything, and it would be useless to try. He seemed to be ever so slightly deaf when someone he disagreed with tried to talk, but he readily noticed and recognized any speaker he wanted to hear. He also had a knack of calling for a vote whenever he sensed that the "wrong" side was gaining momentum.

Several elderly town fathers held the important offices, and most everyone seemed to think of them as Supreme Court–type lifetime appointments. As I came in I heard one man ask another if he planned to stand for any office that year. The other replied, puzzled, "Why, did someone die?"

The day before, Roger and I had planned our visit as best we could without knowing what to expect. We would stand up back, move around a lot, and not miss a thing. Our plans were dashed, however, since each family decided that if clans sat together, all the youthful ones could best be watched.

The first business of the day was a long, boring reading of the warning, as the meeting agenda was called. It had at least two dozen articles to be voted on and was filled with such phrases as "vote to appropriate three cents on the dollar for . . .," and "to instruct the selectmen to . . . ." The reading was followed by the speedy, perennial election of Mr. Wilcox as moderator and the fast reelection, also by voice vote, of the treasurer and the town clerk.

"Next office is that of selectman," called out Mr. Wilcox in his rich Scottish-Yankee twang. "By law this vote has to be by ballot. The term of Hiram B. Calhoon expires at this time. For'd yer ballots." He allowed no time for other nominations or questions, and no one asked if Mr. Calhoon, who had already been a selectman for eighteen years, was interested in another three-year term. The voters dutifully swarmed forward to drop their ballots—usually little pieces of an old calendar sheet they'd brought from home—into the wooden box. Miss Rogers, the assistant town clerk, watched the crowd intently while this was going on and stopped several voters from dropping their choices in the box. They went away rather chagrined as everybody then knew they hadn't paid their $3.35 poll tax.

As soon as the voters returned to their seats, a group of men composing the Board of Civil Authority trouped forward to count them. Then Mr. Wilcox banged his gavel for silence: "Seventy-six ballots cast. Necessary for election, thirty-eight. Mr. Calhoon has seventy-five, therefore he is elected. Next office is that of school director. The term of Agnes Switzer expires at this time. For'd yer ballots." Again, the moderator didn't wait for any opposition.

Only when it came to the vote for road commissioner did the voters interrupt his routine. I had heard a lot of discussion in our neighborhood during the preceding weeks and knew that the farmers were ganging up on the present road commissioner, Ed Christie from the village. They hoped to replace him with one of their own men. Like everyone else, I anxiously waited to see what would happen next, since this vote would likely be the most exciting of the day. Ed Christie sat in the back row, his red plaid shirt stained with tobacco juice and diesel oil. He was surrounded by his road crew, most of whom kept their caps on and their jackets buttoned tight. His jaw was set, as though he anticipated the blast that was coming.

"The term of Ed Christie expires at this time," announced Mr. Wilcox.

"Mr. Moderator," came a loud nasal voice from the far corner of the room before Mr. Wilcox could get out his "for'd" instructions. Taken aback, Wilcox paused and peered toward the voice.

"I nominate Oscar LaForce," continued the man. "Second the nomination," called another. A murmur of surprise swept through the room. Christie's supporters were caught off guard, but someone recovered enough to quickly nominate him, and his name was also seconded. The battle lines were drawn.

For a few seconds the bewildered moderator puzzled over the extraordinary turn of events, unsure of what to do. Here was an unfamiliar situation—an actual contest. Mr. Wilcox seemed to vacillate between calling for a voice vote and having a show of hands. "Ballot, ballot," cried several people, and suddenly it seemed as if everyone was talking at once.

Wilcox banged his gavel a few times. "For'd yer ballots fer road commissioner," he called, and the townspeople quickly surged forward. It took a long time to count and recount the ballots, but finally Oscar was declared the winner, sixty-five to sixty-three. It was a big day for the folks from the back country, and the smiles of the farmers showed it.

The crisis over, the meeting resumed. Christie, thoroughly crushed, sat staring at his town report in a state of shock and didn't get up to vote for the rest of the morning. Gradually the crew of road helpers who had been sitting with him began to drift away. Desperate to hold on to their jobs, they began to gather somewhat uneasily around the newly elected LaForce, who never stopped beaming.

After the elections of the other town officials were completed, the moderator was less hurried. He allowed, and sometimes even seemed to encourage, discussion about schools, roads, cemeteries, and Memorial Day. I noticed that the audience usually nodded agreeably with the smooth-talking, skilled speakers, although sometimes what they said was nonsense. But when a plain-speaking, less eloquent man stood up, he was often snickered at and given little attention, even when he had a terrific idea.

As the account of the Overseer of the Poor was being discussed, Mrs. Noble rose to say that she was not the same June Noble listed in the town report as having received $38.10 from the welfare account. Furthermore, she emphasized, *that* Mrs. Noble was no relation of hers. "I mention this every year," she said in her whiny voice, "and I think that just once the auditors could list her as Mrs. Harvey Noble if they had a mind to." Her remarks were duly noted but not long remembered. She was to make the same speech for the next several years.

Someone brought in word that dinner was ready, and a move to recess quickly passed. "We'll start in exactly one hour. Be on time," warned Mr. Wilcox.

My family and I joined the others at the church next door, where big tables had been set up in the Sunday school rooms. The churchwomen had prepared the meal, which cost thirty cents for grown-ups and twenty cents for children under fifteen. It consisted of all the baked beans, brown bread, potato salad, and casseroles we could eat, and in addition there was coffee, milk, and a piece of the pie of our choice. It was difficult for me to make a decision between pumpkin with whipped cream, blueberry, chocolate cream, rhubarb, raspberry, mince, and raisin. Everyone was very friendly as the food was passed around family style, and a few of those who had said mean things about Ed Christie's care of the back roads went out of their way to talk to him.

When we returned to the hall a bit before the meeting was to start, we saw that someone had taken food to all the officials up front so they could eat at their places. They had been kept busy, because a large group of people came to town meeting during the lunch hour only to vote on whether or not the stores in town should be allowed to sell alcoholic beverages. The men and women, all in their everyday clothes, marched to the front of the hall and climbed the stairs to the stage where two little polling booths had been set up. They voted and promptly left.

After dinner, business went as smooth as ice. Several of the contentious folks who had come, apparently, only to elect a new road commissioner didn't return in the afternoon. The sun came out, everyone was well fed, and each article on the warning passed intact, except for the one that proposed spending an extra $25 for library books.

"Let 'em raise the money theirselves," said a young farmer who was apparently a nonreader. "Leave the village folks do it," muttered someone in our corner, not loud enough for the moderator to hear. "They're the only ones who use the library anyway." The article went down to defeat in spite of a passionate plea by Lillian Austin, one of the library trustees.

Nearly everyone, except the trustees, felt good about finally saving the town some money. They went on to approve the tax rate and to form a committee to investigate burning coal in the village school. Then a member of the Board of Civil Authority rose to say that the polls for voting on the sale of alcoholic beverages would soon close, and if you hadn't voted, you should do it immediately. They then gathered around the front table to sort out the ballots and soon announced that the vote had come out ninety-five against, and sixty-five for. There was a sigh of relief from the crowd that the favored side had once more prevailed, and the town would be dry for one more year. Mrs. MacDonald, in back of me, whispered to her neighbor with great concern that the opposition seemed to be getting more powerful each year. She remember that a few years back there had been only eighteen votes for the wets.

Then the gavel fell, and the moderator declared the meeting adjourned. We got home for chores with the events of the day destined to occupy our conversation for the next few days. The speeches that the men in our neighborhood had promised all winter were still unmade, but we knew that the grumblings about the village folk and the ways of local government would continue in the back country until the next town meeting.

I felt lucky that there had been enough excitement to give me something to report in class the next day. Still, as the three of us from District 9 School compared notes while going down the stairs, we agreed that it hadn't been as lively as we'd hoped. The year before, we'd heard, Jed Hollister, a toothless farmer from the east side of town, had gotten mighty riled at some of the statements Arthur King, one of the village cusses, was making. He got out of his seat, marched over, and gave the speaker a hard kick in the seat of the pants. Jed hadn't shown up for town meeting this year.

SUGAR AND MUD

By early April we rejoiced at any sign of spring we could find, although usually there weren't many. Mrs. Cheever always noted that the sun, which she had recorded as rising at a quarter of eight during the first week of January, was now coming over the mountain at a quarter of six. Emma Finney contributed the encouragement that the afternoon sun had started to shine in her back kitchen windows for a few minutes just before it went down. But the robins had not yet ventured back from the south, and the daffodils knew better than to push through the snow that still covered the ground.

One year, the first week in April we were cheered when a sure sign appeared. We had just come in from the barn for breakfast when we heard a knock on the door, and there was Lavina Enfield standing on our veranda, red-cheeked and somewhat out of breath. Although 7:30 in the morning was not an unusual time for a neighboring farmer to drop by, Mrs. Enfield lived six miles away and had no visible means of conveyance with her.

My mother invited her in for breakfast, apologizing for the "terrible mess the house is in," meaning that the muffin tins were still unwashed in the sink. Mrs. Enfield pulled up a chair, joined us at the table, and told us that she just got the urge to go "crust walking."

"I got so plumb sick of not seeing a body for so long, I up and lit out," she said, explaining that she had started well before sunrise and taken the three-mile shortcut over Baker Hill. "I warn't even sure where I would end up. Would have stopped at Effie Jones's, but their dog barked at me, so I cut right by there."

As she devoured a big bowl of oatmeal, a cup of coffee, and several graham rolls, Lavina glowingly and in great detail described the winter's activities on her side of the hill. She made a lot of inquiries about the doin's in our neighborhood, too, and as I left for school, she seemed ready to spend the day. I learned later that she had stayed so long, fretting to herself that she'd never make it home before the crust softened, that my mother stopped enjoying her visit. Since she had no telephone, it was several days before we heard that she'd made it with no difficulty. She had kept to the woods and high country where the snow stayed hard longer, and apparently the six-mile trek did her no harm.

According to the older members of my family, in earlier days there had been a lot of crust walking. The women, who had been shut in all winter, especially welcomed the chance to hightail it crosslots to visit folks who themselves hadn't seen an outsider for months. Even the long skirts they wore at the turn of the century apparently didn't hinder walking on the frozen snow. The important thing was to be aware of the time and, like Cinderella, not to tarry.

Lonely people were not the only ones to take advantage of the hard crust. Our dogs, cats, geese, and even the wild animals frolicked on it. Farmers drove their horses over the firm surface to spread manure in the fields and scatter their buckets for sugaring. Hunters and trappers used crust to get into the back country easily, and woodsmen explored remote forest lots. Sometimes they forgot to take snowshoes and stayed too long. Each spring we heard of some poor soul floundering out of the woods long after dark. Usually he collapsed at a farmhouse, exhausted and soaked to the hide from wading through miles of hip-deep wet snow.

At school we loved feeling free, once again, to run through the fields and woods, play games, and slide and roll on the crust. Sometimes four or five of us got on the long narrow traverse sled that Robert Coomer had dragged a mile and a half to school. We tore down the hills at neck-breaking speed, dodging trees and rocks and more than once tipping over and bloodying our faces on the icy snow.

Though it was harder to mark the course properly, Fox and Geese was much easier to play on the crust than it had been in the deep snow. This slightly more complicated game of tag always replaced Prisoner's Base and Anti-Over for the winter, and we played it every day when the weather permitted. We tracked out a square about 100 feet on each side with diagonal paths from corner to corner. In the center stood the fox, ready to catch the players called the geese, who were safe only when they were on the corner bases. Since four bases were too few for a dozen or so geese, a winding tail, about fifty feet long, was made from the first square to a second, similar layout that was circular and much smaller. This one was called the "pie." A player could run out on the circle when things got too crowded or dull on the big square.

Tempting the fox was the fun of the game, and the geese were expected to run continually from base to base. Usually a fast runner was chosen to be the fox for the first game, since the odds were against him. The last kid to be tagged became the fox for the next game.

By noon recess, sometimes the snow had softened enough so that we could roll big snowballs into fortlike structures, and we had rousing snowball fights. As in Prisoner's Base, the teams were labeled from our history lessons. Snowball fights often ended with someone crying as a wet snowball caught him smack in the face and spattered down his neck.

In spite of the outdoor games and the fun of dropping snow down the girls' necks, we all looked forward eagerly to spring vacation. Except for Washington's Birthday, we hadn't had a day off from school since New Year's, so the upcoming weeks in April were eagerly anticipated.

We couldn't count the days until vacation, however, because it was always declared during mud season. No one could guess when that might occur, or how long it would last, but we could usually count on a three-week recess at least. It took a long time to melt the snow that had been packed in the roads all winter by the rollers, and it was always many weeks after we returned to school before the mud dried out completely. Our roads were of dirt, not gravel, and each year the road machine scraped them lower and lower to make them smooth. Consequently, most of the water from the surrounding area ran into them, and each year we would see someone standing helplessly by his car as it sank deeper and deeper into the gooey slime.

Because even the horses couldn't move easily during mud weeks, we planned ahead and in late winter stockpiled flour, white sugar, kerosene, grain for the chickens and cattle, and other heavy supplies. We sent our orders to Sears Roebuck and Montgomery Ward in early February because the mailman often couldn't get to the back country for a couple of weeks or more in the springtime. All the men and boys and some of the women got a new pair of high rubber boots each spring for sugaring, and we wore them most of the time until the mud was gone.

Long before every muddy spot in the roads had dried out, people tried to drive over them and got stuck. Some of the village folks told stories about farmers who earned lots of money by using their horses all day to pull the cars through a large mud hole in front of their house, then spent most of the night hauling water to make more mud for the next day. It never happened in our neighborhood, or probably anywhere else. People grumbled a lot about the "town folks who didn't know any better than to run the roads before they oughta," but they pulled them out when they got stuck and never charged a cent. We were all told frequently that it wasn't right to make a profit off someone else's misfortune.

Another reason for a long spring vacation was the maple sugar season. All schoolchildren were expected to work in their parents' or someone else's sugar place each spring. Even before the sugar season actually arrived we knew it was coming, because on warm days we would find sap icicles hanging from broken branches on the maple trees that grew near the schoolhouse. They made deliciously sweet popsicles to suck on.

The woods and sugar house smelled far better than the stable and the pig pen and were much more pleasant places in which to work. At an early age I was thoroughly convinced that maple syrup furiously boiling in a pan presented the prettiest sight and the sweetest smell on Earth.

Sap runs best when the days are warm and the nights below freezing. We had to be ready for the first run because some years the season was very short. Although sugaring was fun, it was also hard work. We scattered a thousand buckets, placing one near each medium-sized tree and two beside the larger ones. Our sugar house, like everyone else's, was built at the bottom of the grove, so the heavy loads of sap could be drawn downhill. Of course, the buckets had to be hauled uphill, and we used a hand sled to drag them in years when the snow was too deep for our horses to navigate.

Each tree was tapped on its east or south side so the sun's warmth could make the sap start to run early in the day. My brothers always hunted for a solid spot of wood where a tap hadn't been made in recent years, and with a hand-cranked brace-and-bit they drilled a hole about an inch deep in the tree. My job was to pound in a metal spout with a hook on it, hang the bucket on the hook, and put a cover on the bucket. Before I was big enough to help, my family had used wooden buckets and covers that my grandfather had made. The brightly painted red, green, and blue buckets made the sugar house colorful, but the State Health Board decided that the lead in the paint didn't do the syrup any good, so every producer had been required to change to metal buckets.

Usually as we were making our preparations, we looked for "sugar snow," super-large flakes of wet snow that fall in such density that visibility is impossible. Some farmers called these snows "line storms" and said that they marked the division between winter and spring.

Before the first sap run, we tipped over the two evaporator pans and rinsed off a year's accumulation of dust. These pans were then set over the furnace, called an arch, and used to boil down the sap to a thin syrup. We always finished boiling it to the proper consistency in a smaller pan and arch. The smaller rig was also used occasionally to boil the syrup down still further to make maple sugar. Our evaporator was nearly new, and my brothers were very proud of it and the "fancy" grade syrup that we made. Frequently they pointed out to me the stone fireplace in the woods near our sugar house; there our ancestors had first boiled sap in a big iron kettle during the early 1800s.

We also scrubbed out the enormous wooden sap storage tub and put up the heavy black smokestack. The preparation took a couple of days, and by then the buckets were often full enough so that we could collect the sap and begin to boil. Usually a frozen crust allowed us to walk around easily in the early morning, but by noon the bright spring sun had softened it, and we had to wallow in soft, mushy snow that might be anywhere from a few inches to four feet deep.

Our two strong black horses pulled the sled and metal sap tank. We dumped the buckets of sap into large wooden gathering pails that we then carried to the tank. When the tank began to slop over, we drove to the sugar house and unloaded the sap with a spout in the back of the tank, letting it run through a long hollowed-out log that led to the wooden storage tub in the sugar house.

It was a wet job, because the deep snow often came over the top of our boots, and since I was short, I occasionally spilled sap into mine when I was dumping a bucket into the high tank on the sled. We got a chance to dry our clothes a little between loads while the sap was running from the tank into the storage tub. I liked backing up to the front of the red-hot arch and watching the steam pour from my wet clothes. The blazing monster kept the building as hot as a foundry, even on cold, windy days.

Maple sap consists of about 40 parts water to one part

syrup, so on the days we made a 50-gallon barrel of syrup, we had to boil away approximately 2,000 gallons of water. The process took an enormous amount of wood, and my brother who did the boiling had to stoke the fire every few minutes. He also had to test the syrup to see if it was ready for drawing off, so he was kept very hot and busy. Large amounts of dark smoke poured from the smokestack, and white steam rose high in the air from the cupola. From our hilltop on a clear spring day we could keep track of the syrup-making operations of seven or eight neighbors.

Sometimes I'd help my brother in the sugar house on rainy days. We took our lunch, and we boiled eggs in the sap and baked potatoes in the hot ashes beneath the fire. During the season, I always ate a hefty amount of the sweet stuff, not only devouring samples taken from the boiling pan but also, like everyone else, pouring fresh syrup on my morning oatmeal each day and frequently having sugar on snow in the evening. Sometimes we had dishes of syrup for dessert at supper and ate lots of sugar cakes and maple cream. Because of the intensely active physical work, we burned up the calories, so it probably did no harm; and I developed an insatiable sweet tooth. Much as I liked syrup, though, I never became as addicted as Uncle Arthur, who poured it over nearly everything he ate, including mashed potatoes, macaroni, sausage, and apple pie.

We no longer "sugared off" and sold maple sugar in tubs by the time I was in school. Instead, like most other farmers, we sold our syrup in fifty-gallon metal drums. Memories of the old "sugaring off" days remained, however. We had an old metal horn hanging on a sugarhouse rafter, and my brothers warned me not to blow it. In past years it had been used as a signal for a sugaring off, and everyone within hearing distance, knowing they were invited, would come running.

The year I was eleven, the Cheevers decided to revive the custom. They had told everyone in advance about the party, but they blew the horn anyway. At the sound of their toots, we banked our fire, ran in enough sap so the evaporator wouldn't boil dry, put the horses in the barn, and started off on the mile-long hike to their woods.

Everyone liked the Cheevers, so we knew there would be a crowd there. Both Fred and Effie were descended from old Scottish families that had come to town a hundred years earlier, and they were real Vermonters in their conversation as well as their attitudes. Effie salted her talk with expressions like "Fiddle" and "Oh, beans" and often reported she'd been "working all day in a bushel basket," meaning what she'd done hadn't amounted to much. When asked her plans for the afternoon, she might say, "Pile up everything I did this fore-noon, and then jump over it." If some matter needed imme-diate attention, Effie said, "It 'pears to be time to stir our stumps." When taking leave of someone she'd say, "See you on a rainy Tuesday," or something similar.

About two dozen people were already there when we arrived. Most were men and boys, but a few women and girls had braved a long hike in the mushy snow, too. The Webster brothers from down in the valley were inspecting the foam-ing golden brew as it boiled near the top of the pan. They all had enormous noses, and the three men looked like the witches from *Macbeth* as they hung over it, periodically warn-ing Effie to pour a bit of milk into the syrup if it was about to boil over.

The Cheevers had filled a dozen wooden sap buckets with snow, and as soon as Effie was satisfied that the golden liquid was thick enough, Fred began to dip it from the pan with a giant shiny tin dipper and pour it onto the buckets of snow. We each took one of the little wooden paddles they provided and eagerly devoured the delicious sugar, which was made even more tasty by the unfamiliar paddles, the fragrant balsam needles mixed with the snow, the crisp spring air, and the competition of the other eaters. Fred had diffi-culty keeping up with the appetites of the hungry crowd and finally decided he was losing the battle. He took his dipper and, with the base of it, pounded down a clean snowbank and poured syrup on it for us kids.

Eventually, though, Fred and Effie had a chance to eat a little sugar themselves while everyone drank large amounts of the water they had provided. Finally, after exchanging a little more news, we all said our "Much obligeds" and sloshed home through the melting snow to finish our day's work. It was a novel experience for me, and I wondered why "sugaring off" had ever gone out of style.

We knew the season was nearing the end when snow in the maple woods finally melted, the nights warmed, and sap took on the taste of maple buds. The final signal each year came when a woodpecker came and banged loudly on the metal smokestack. Then it was time to gather the last run of sap, called the "frog run" or "bud run," and boil it into a dark thin syrup. This was poured into an oak barrel in our cellar, where it turned into sap vinegar. We used quantities of it each year for making a wide variety of items, including pickles, salad dressing, horseradish, and cough syrup, and we poured it generously over fresh dandelion greens, chard, and lettuce.

At the end of the sugar season came the long, messy job of cleaning up. We had to pick up all the buckets and spouts and wash them with soap flakes and hot water, as well as scrub out the boiling pans, gathering tank, and storage tub. Finally we took down the heavy smokestack, cleaned the ashes out of the arch, and put away the sleds until the next year.

Along with the sugar season came tempting puddles that were wonderful to wade through in my new boots. The puddles were invariably deeper than I'd thought, and I regularly came home with wet feet in spite of my mother's admonitions. I usually caught the cold she predicted, too, thus unfortunately reminding her that it was time for the annual spring tonic.

Like the mothers of all my schoolmates, Ma had her own methods of warding off spring illnesses. She agreed with the popular notion that, because we spent so much of the winter indoors and ate foods that were stored and canned instead of fresh, our bodies needed a good "flushing out," like an old drainpipe, come spring. After the purge, the body then had to be "dosed up" with a good tonic so we would get going on the spring work.

Luckily, I was born late, and my family had given up the traditional spring slug of sulfur mixed with molasses. Some of my schoolmates were still so treated, however, and described the procedure with great disgust. In spite of the fact that all winter I had been dosed with cod liver oil, Ma felt that spring definitely called for what was commonly referred to in our region as a "physic."

Her favorite was senna, a terrible-tasting tea brewed from plants grown in Egypt and sold in every country store. Because it was such a powerful laxative, it could be drunk only on weekends when one wasn't in school. Senna was followed by daily doses of Hood's Sasparilla, a brown, root-flavored substance that some old-timers enjoyed saying was also an aphrodisiac. It was reputed to cleanse the innards and tone up the blood and humours. No one seemed to know what humours actually were, but from an old book I learned that there were supposed to be four of them. Anyway, it was courting ruination to face spring without having them all in good shape.

We all detested the tonics and would have preferred to take a chance with whatever the alternative might be. Each year I hoped that Ma would forget the ritual, but whenever she did, Grammy Corkins or Miz Coomer were sure to remind her. Until we were out of grade school, the spring "fix" was an annual ritual, and I gratefully noted that when I'd finally outgrown it, no scourge had overtaken me.

Many older folks in our neighborhood touted other tonics that I thought made more sense. Hiram Wright said that drinking several gallons of maple sap every March got him going. Joe Waugh touted birch sap as being even better for what ailed him, and Grammie Jones said that her family never felt really perky until she served them the first mess of dandelion greens. Jack Reynolds advised spreading fresh grated horseradish on everything from potatoes to boiled cider pie.

My own favorite spring tonic was the one recommended by my Uncle Henry. It consisted of a cup of freshly boiled maple syrup, cooled slightly in a snowbank, and drunk very slowly while it was just slightly below the boiling point. It seemed the perfect way to end a bitter cold winter and a long depressing mud season, and served as an invigorating sweet toast to the rapidly arriving spring.

RECESS

In spite of the hard work of sugaring, spring vacation always passed far too quickly, and by late April we were back in school. Each year, it was always a shock to find how much different my classmates looked after the three or four weeks of separation. Everyone seemed to have grown an inch or so, and we had shed our heavy clothes. Since we hadn't worn our shoes since October, we had outgrown them, so most of us were breaking in a pair of new ones. Even though they were a welcome change from the heavy rubber boots, they were far from comfortable. New shoes were always extremely stiff and didn't ever quite fit, so wearing them was a form of slow torture. For at least a week they felt as if they were made of wood, and they always squeaked loudly. We could readily identify who had new shoes, not only by the squeak but also by the slight limp of the owner.

The new shoes were always noticed and commented upon, and if by chance one forgot to mention them, the proud wearer usually pointed them out and displayed the painful little blisters already forming on his feet. The soles of the shoes were nailed on rather than sewn, so we could also expect the little nails to begin to work their way into our feet within a few days, too. These were very painful until we could get to a hammer and pound them over so they wouldn't hurt.

For the first time in many months we played games at recess and the noon hour on bare ground. As usual, the older kids were in charge, choosing which games to play, picking the players, and refereeing all the close decisions. The teacher appeared on the playground only to stop a fight, give first aid, or to announce with her clanging bell that recess was over.

We played baseball from time to time, but the favorite game was once again Prisoner's Base, the one that had confused me so much on my first day at school. As usual we chose sides by calling our teams the Settlers against the Indians, Germans against the Allies, or the Sailors against the Pirates, depending on which war the leaders were studying in their history lesson at the time. Occasionally we played girls against the boys or the older children against the younger.

The teams lined up, facing each other, as in a game of football. The idea in Prisoner's Base was to run to the goal post that was located at the far end of the opposing team's territory, and as long as you touched it you were safe. On the way to and from it you could be tagged and taken prisoner. Anyone scoring a goal by touching the post without getting caught could rescue a prisoner. No one ever kept score, so unless an entire team was taken prisoner, no side ever won. It was just lively exercise, with lots of action.

Anti-Over was another game that created a great deal of running and yelling, at which we excelled. Two teams were picked, as in Prisoner's Base. One group was positioned on one side of the schoolhouse, and one on the other. A boy or girl then threw a soft rubber ball over the building, and everyone on the team yelled "anti-over." When someone on the other team caught the ball, he or she hid it behind his back, and the whole team ran to the other side of the building, some running one way, and some the other. The child who was carrying the ball tagged as many of the opposing team as possible before they escaped, and they had to join his side. The untagged members ran to the other side of the building, and the game resumed.

Anti-Over was fun, but it often resulted in bruised heads as we all reached for the ball. Because we were lousy catchers, changing sides was not frequent, and the game was hard on the wooden shingles that covered the schoolhouse roof.

I Spy, which was what we called Hide and Seek, was another of our favorites, and many schoolchildren learned to count by being "it." Usually we counted to 30 by ones, or to 50 by twos or to 100 by fives. Tug-of-War, Tag, walking on the board fence that surrounded our yard, and climbing up the swing posts all helped disperse the energy accumulated as we sat in the classroom.

Occasionally one of us would demonstrate a trick seen at the fair and practiced at home. Jack Hudson, from time to time, attempted to balance an upright broom on his forehead, juggle rocks, walk on his hands, or perform some other enviable feat. Brad Lincoln's big thing was to shinny up the swing poles and come back down fast, head first.

One year, with the money earned at our Halloween party, the teacher bought a basketball and basket for the schoolyard. Because none of us had ever seen a basketball game, we didn't get too excited about playing it ourselves. As one boy put it, "You throw it up, and it either goes in the basket or it doesn't." It was a cheap ball, and when it went flat for the third time no one bothered to patch it and blow it up again.

Every spring we always lost one recess to Arbor Day. The state government designated a special day for the event, and every country school was expected to plant a tree. Since northern Vermont lagged considerably behind most of the state as far as spring was concerned, on the officially proclaimed day we usually had at least two feet of snow on the ground.

Our teachers felt that a tree-planting ceremony was too important to miss, however. So when the snow had melted and the ground thawed, we observed Arbor Day. Important though it was, for some reason the teachers always felt that the ceremony should not take place during class time, so we lost either a recess or part of our noon hour because of it.

Somehow the teachers always acquired a maple or poplar tree for the occasion. The tree was usually about seven feet tall, rather spindly, with very few roots. After long discussion, a spot was selected where an eighty-foot specimen would look nice in future years.

None of us, although we were growing up on farms, knew anything about planting a tree. Trees grew everywhere, and nobody had to plant them. The new tree was invariably left lying on the ground, its roots bare and drying in the sun, while someone read a lengthy and pompous decree from the governor. We sang a patriotic song or two, and one pupil in the seventh or eighth grade always recited "Trees" by Joyce Kilmer. Finally, after hearing the promises of "nests of robins in her hair," we planted our tree in the far-too-small hole we had dug. No one considered wasting any of our precious water on it, and our tree, carelessly placed in the lifeless clay soil, packed hard from a century of pounding feet, had no more chance of survival than a Puritan preacher at a Mafia convention. We had a good spot for planting a tree at the following year's ceremony, though, when another conscientious teacher would interrupt another baseball game.

Actually it wouldn't be fair to call our game "baseball." After watching a spirited game, one cynical teacher said it was enough to make the bushes laugh. As soon as the mud dried up, or a little before, we took our ball, bat, and well-worn gloves into the schoolyard. If anyone accidentally caught the ball or hit it more than seventy-five feet, there was a lot of excitement. Although none of us knew much about the game, and we played strictly by our own rules, we had heard about Babe Ruth and Joe DiMaggio and imagined that we played quite a lot like them. Games never moved very fast, because we owned only one old beat-up ball, and a lot of time was spent hunting for it in the bushes or fishing it out of mudholes in the swamp beside the school.

One summer three of us happened to be at the county fair on its baseball day. The players were from neighboring towns and worked in garages, or were store clerks, millhands, or truck drivers who played baseball every weekend all summer for the fun of it. But if they had been two teams of professionals, we couldn't have been more impressed.

We watched open-mouthed at the speed with which they played, the accuracy and force with which they hit the ball, their straight throws, and their sure catches. Even two youthful Boy Scouts playing toss on the sidelines seemed to catch every throw unerringly. We went home inspired, determined to become real baseball players.

At school that fall, we tried to improve our skill, but our schoolmates who hadn't seen the game (especially the girls) were less enthusiastic. Although diligent practice improved our catches a bit, disinterest won out, and we spent the fall recesses playing our old brand of baseball and the other games that students in our school had played for decades.

We formed clubs, built hideouts out of the bushes and small trees that grew around the nearby stone walls, and made tree houses in the big maples across the road. We played Indians, making our bows out of birch saplings and whittling white cedar arrows that never seemed to shoot straight. When the bark was slippery in the spring, we carved whistles from the soft wood of the poplars and made blowguns from the horrible-tasting elder bushes.

If a boy was discovered walking around with his trousers unbuttoned, no one ever mentioned it outright. The girls would giggle and some boy would yell, "Hey, it's one o'clock," alerting him and everyone else to the situation. No girl was ever told that her petticoat was showing, either. Instead, someone always said, "It's snowy down south."

In the schoolyard, a sportsmanlike code of regulations had developed over the years. No cheating was allowed under any circumstances, and the older kids quickly punched anyone who broke that rule. Serious fights, though, were fairly rare, and no one ever got badly hurt. One fall, however, the peaceful recesses came to an end when two new boys named Pat and Mike moved into our neighborhood. Although they were only seven and eight years old, they were the most belligerent kids we had ever seen. They had jet black hair and heavy eyebrows and claimed to smoke and chew tobacco at home. They swore violently, scowled all the time, and sneered at our invitations to join in the games. Both seemed bent on proving that they were as tough as they looked.

Before their first week in school was over, they'd had a knock-down, bloody-nose fight with every boy in school, from little Stephen Rice to big, rugged, mild-mannered Leopaul Lapointe. Every boy had a black eye, and the teacher was becoming alarmed at the speed with which the first aid kit was being depleted so early in the year. Gradually we learned that the only way to handle them was for several of us to gang up and sit on them until they promised to behave. When this happened, they quickly agreed, but unfortunately the good behavior lasted for only a few minutes before we were all at it again. At the end of the second week, they still gave no sign whatever of becoming civilized, but fortunately their parents abruptly moved back to the town from which they'd come. We were all happy. Recess returned to normal, and we once again played our games in comparative peace.

Even more than the teacher, Rose and Lily Barker acted as our consciences during most of my school years, and they did their best to keep us acting the way they thought we should, especially during recesses. We boys got very tired of their habit of pointing an accusing finger at us and saying "Vaw," a Yankee term meaning shame. They wore clean starched dresses every day and refused to play the most active games, fearing they would get them dirty. They called attention to anyone they thought was doing something they shouldn't and tattled all our misdeeds to the teacher.

Because they were girls we couldn't sock them, so we had to think up other ways of getting even. One of our most successful ploys was to make them think we were doing something bad, like smoking, starting a fire, or planning some other devilment they weren't sure enough about to tell the teacher. It always drove them wild.

Roger Lincoln and I were good friends for most of my school years. The winter I was twelve and he was thirteen, we decided to be Boy Scouts like those we had read about in *The Boy Scouts with the Allies, The Boy Scouts on the Trail,*

The Boy Scouts to the Rescue, and countless others. Roger was a much better Scout than I and went so fully prepared he could barely walk. His pockets were full of things like waterproof matches, a pocket knife, a coil of heavy string, a compass, a magnifying glass for starting fires, a whistle, a mirror for signaling, a pencil, and much more. We learned the Morse code and wigwag signals, and we made elaborate plans to build a cabin in the woods and a boat as soon as summer came. We drew maps and carefully detailed all the secret spots where we would go on survival trips; send smoke signals to each other from hills miles apart; eat fish, berries, and small animals; and spend hours hunting for the buried treasure that some man who never returned from the Civil War was supposed to have hidden.

By the time school was out, both Roger's family and mine had other plans for us, unfortunately, and since we lived nearly three miles apart, I didn't see him all summer except for an occasional Sunday afternoon. The messages went unsent, and as far as I know, the treasure is still there.

Charlie Forge's high imagination kept many recesses from being dull. He read every word in the current event papers our school received during my last two years. He also listened to his family's radio (whenever it worked) and became fascinated with everything happening in the world. Sometimes he organized us into fifth-column mercenaries in Spain, G-men chasing bank robbers and kidnappers, or Hitler Youth. One winter day he talked us all into climbing up on the woodshed roof and then further up onto the schoolhouse for a hair-raising, bone-jarring paratrooper attack down into the enemy's snow fort.

During one period of labor unrest in Detroit, under Charlie's leadership we became part of what must have been one of the shortest strikes in history. After talking about it for a day or two, one recess we made big signs on old calendar pads that read, "Miss Reynolds is Unfair" and "We Demand Shorter Hours and Longer Vacations." Banging loudly on big metal drums that once contained dust repellent for the floor, every pupil in school started to march around the building.

Usually our teachers took little interest in our recess activities, so we were surprised when, as we passed the window where Miss Reynolds was correcting papers, she seemed to be getting excited. Tearing out of the building at close to the speed of a flying bullet, she brought the parade to an abrupt halt and speedily ordered us all inside. There we stayed, not only for the rest of that recess but also for all recesses for the rest of the week. We were stunned because we liked Miss Reynolds and didn't expect to be taken so seriously. Our imprisonment did make us examine Charlie's ideas more closely, and Myrtle Waugh said that if our teacher had been in charge of labor relations, we probably never would have heard of John L. Lewis.

NORTH COUNTRY WEATHER

Nearly every grown-up I knew was a weather prophet. Their predications relied heavily on a series of signs ranging from a flare-up of Aunt Liz's rheumatism to seeing a cat wash her face on the veranda, both of which indicated it would rain soon. Our local prognosticators' low rate of success didn't discourage them a bit, and they never gave up predicting bad winters, dry decades, and not-so-good weather for the next day.

The moon figured heavily in Mark Coomer's predictions. "Change of moon, change of weather," he said frequently. Surprisingly, he was often right. He predicted a frost on the full moon each June, and we learned to cover our tomato plants according to his warnings. A full moon in April, according to Mark, invariably brought a run of sap, though this didn't always happen. Over and over again, I heard from him and others that a circle around the moon meant a big storm was coming, and the number of stars inside the circle indicated the days of grace we had to get ready for the event. A crescent moon, flat like a Venetian gondola, meant we had a dry season ahead; and one tipped up on the side indicated that water could run out of it easily, so we'd better expect a rainy time.

Everyone agreed that a mackerel or buttermilk sky meant we'd have a storm within a few days, as did the high-flying, wispy mare's tail clouds. There were many signs in the summer that warned us to get the hay into the barn quickly so it would not get wet: a red sunrise, the clear hollow sound of the mill whistle down in the Bend, a sudden change of wind direction, birds sitting on the telephone wires, the cows lying down in a group, and spots on the palm of your hand. On the other hand, red sunsets, late-afternoon rainbows, high-flying barn swallows, smoke rising high in the air, and a light, steady north wind were all indications of good weather ahead. Many of these predictions were easy to accept because they could be explained scientifically.

Some other predictions were harder for me to believe. Effie Cheever made her long-range forecasts by the calendar. "The last Friday of each month governs the weather for the following month," she claimed knowingly. Grammy Johnson went her one better. She always forecast the weather for the entire year by observing the twelve days of Christmas. "Each day is an indication of what the corresponding month will be like," she declared. In her presence one day I wondered aloud whether, if a big blizzard were to hit on the sixth, seventh, and eighth days, we should expect snowy weather throughout June, July, and August. I was quickly told, "Shush your nonsense."

Steely Lincoln agreed with Effie that the "twelve days" system was a proper indicator of weather for the upcoming year, but they disagreed about how to count the days. Steely felt that you should count Christmas as the first day, but Effie maintained you should begin with the day after, and not count any Sundays.

Uncle Calvin Jardine, one of the most loyal Republicans who ever walked the hills of Vermont, claimed that the Democrats were to blame for each poor season we'd had since the 1932 election. He said things weren't likely to improve until the scalawags were voted out. He had a lot of support around the neighborhood for his theory, but Widow Haines, who was old enough to argue with him, pointed out that there were dry summers and harsh winters when she was a girl and Lincoln was president. Cal retorted, "Those were more'n likely caused by the war."

Uncle Cal had so much fun blaming the Roosevelt administration for everything, I wondered what he'd done for amusement while Hoover had been president. He never mentioned F.D.R. by name, always referring to "that man," or "that scoundrel in the White House." I asked him once why he never used the president's name, and he said it was "too much gol' 'ram trouble to rinse my mouth out afterward." He also carefully never credited the administration for any of the beautiful days, apparently feeling that they'd slipped by in spite of the rascals.

Whenever Yankees gathered, weather discussion supplied nearly as much conversation as gossip. The newfangled radio waves got a lot of blame for our bad days, as did having telephone wires strung all over Creation. Airplanes and automobiles ramming around the countryside were suspected to cause poor weather, too.

Ralph Twist maintained that our dry summers were caused because the farmers had stopped using straw for bedding in their barns and instead used sawdust, which they then spread on their fields. "Dries out all the soil and the air, too," he claimed. Snort Finney declared that the drought was caused because the Pullock Paper Company had cut the lumber off most of Wheelock Mountain. Wilbur Vogelman blamed the war in Spain. Others claimed it was caused by the new French-Canadian farmers' burning so much brush while clearing their land, by the Nazis' trying out a new death ray that would eventually kill off everybody, or by the damn summer people who seemed possessed to run motorboats day after day on the lake.

The biggest proportion of our neighbors, however, felt that most bad weather was caused by the Lord, who was punishing His errant children. Judah MacDougal felt that the sinful city visitors running around half naked all summer caused a lot of the trouble, but most folks set the blame nearer home. Everyone's waywardness was carefully observed and remembered, so we would know where to properly fix the blame when necessary. If Walter Gamble got in a load of hay on Sunday, which he did occasionally when he thought no one was watching, we all knew we could expect rain for the rest of the week.

Although I couldn't understand why Walter's sinning ought to inflict bad weather on the rest of us, I half believed, like everyone else, that it did. I remember feeling very unkindly toward Emma Finney while I was shoveling a foot of heavy, wet snow off the chicken house roof in early May. She'd had, we were told, the poor judgment to hang out her wash on a Sabbath morning.

Only Fred Cheever in his slow, deliberate way seemed to live contentedly with the weather. We used to watch him, and when he mowed down ten acres of oats, we felt sure it wouldn't rain for a week. We asked him once how he guessed correctly every time.

"Never pay no mind to the radio predictions, moon signs, or all the stuff folks tell you," he'd say. "Just do your mowin' when it feels right in your bones, and never look up."

Many farmers had weathervanes on their barns and watched them closely for some indication of what to expect. Most of the year, the wind came out of the north or northwest and ranked somewhere between cool and bitter cold. We knew it dried the hay, the washing, and the spring mud, but it blew shingles off the roof and panes of glass out of the barn windows and rearranged everything else, too. Now and then we found some interesting object that had blown in from a neighbor's yard, and probably they received some of our things that disappeared, too. Old Roy Temple claimed that the wind took off his hat in a gust one Monday morning, blew it against the side of the barn, and it was still there at noon on Saturday.

John McLaren made good use of the wind. He had a windmill about fifty feet tall that pumped water for his house and barn, and he was the only person I knew who grumbled about prolonged calm spells. Walter Gamble on Wheelock Mountain used it, too. He had on his roof a six-volt windcharger that supplied power both for his radio and the automobile headlight he used for a reading lamp. When we could see his light glowing three miles away on a dark night, we knew the wind was blowing and he was happily listening to Lum 'n' Abner, Eddie Cantor, or the Andrews Sisters.

Grammy Twist rang up her son Ralph one cold March morning, and told him he'd better begin getting ready for sugaring that day. "Notice we got a good south wind for a change," she observed.

"Feels to me like it's the north wind coming back," Ralph retorted with good old Yankee pessimism.

Although they didn't always admit it, everyone was afraid of the hard thundershowers that often struck our mountains. Even the sturdier grown-ups looked very uncomfortable during a rough storm, although they tried to bluff it out in front of others. We had a rough old character named Mike as a hired man for a few months one summer, and he made a big deal about how tough he was. Although he denounced God, the Church, and Satan with equal verve, we noticed that he always turned white and stopped swearing during thunderstorms.

Like many other families in the hills, we'd once had a barn struck and burned by lightning, and over the years we lost several cows and a horse. Many elm and pine trees on our property had dead tops and had had bark stripped off by lightning, and one of our fields had a large hole in it from a strike. One scary night when I was about six, a dead maple tree not far from my window was struck. I watched as it burned for most of the night, and it made an indelible impression on me. We had all heard many times the story of the Barker boys, who had been sitting near the stove one evening when lightning struck their chimney. It knocked them both on their backs and started a small fire in the attic.

Ma always routed us out of bed during a night thunderstorm, since she felt that upstairs was not a good place to be. We always dressed, ready to flee if we had to, and she made us sit in a "safe" place. It was considered hazardous to be near a stove, chimney, window, door, or water pipe. In our small house that didn't leave many safe spots.

Snort and Emma Finney had heard that rubber was a

good insulator, so they always sat in their car during a storm. Some mothers made their children put on their boots and stand up. Molly Forge had read that glass stopped electricity, so she placed a kitchen chair in four drinking glasses and sat on it, tucking her feet up under her.

Using any metal object during a storm was considered hazardous, and plenty of stories proved how dangerous it could be. Not only were pitchforks forbidden, but also knitting needles, scissors, silverware, knives, and even fountain pens. There wasn't much we could do during a storm except try to remember all the bad things we had done and pray hard for forgiveness.

Most of our worst storms came in mid-summer, so when we had one at school in late May, it surprised everyone. We had the first inkling that something big was stirring when the schoolroom suddenly began to get dark. We looked at one another and at the clock. It was only three.

We knew that thunderstorms could be mighty unpredictable. Sometimes we would hear thunder knocking around in the west for hours, and it would never hit our area at all. Other times a storm would barrel in on us with alarming speed, catching people in the hayfield, in the middle of the lake in a rowboat, or deep in the woods searching for a lost cow.

For the first time, Miss Goodrich looked worried as she stared out the window. The western sky, which had been pleasantly blue during the noon hour, had turned very black. Then we heard the first roll of distant thunder, and before anyone could suggest closing school early, lightning flashed in the dark sky, and the first large drops of rain banged against the windows. Then the storm began, loud and terrifying.

We moved away from the windows, as we had often been warned to do, and closed the door. Each boom of thunder made us jump higher, and because we were holding our breath with fear, our bodies became weak and chilly. I looked at the teacher and older kids for reassurance, but they appeared just as concerned as I. We all knew the schoolhouse didn't have lightning rods and that it stuck up like a bandaged thumb, the only tall object between two fields. We all felt certain that with the next boom we would be disintegrated as if by a giant cherry bomb.

The teacher tried to help. "Don't forget the school has been here for a hundred years, and it hasn't been hit once," she told us.

"Lightning never strikes twice in the same place," volunteered Kate Hudson weakly, also bravely trying to lift our spirits, but failing miserably.

Suddenly there was a boom that made all the other tremendous crashes pale by comparison. We knew for certain that the end had come.

"It hit the barn. I saw it," cried Charlie Forge. We ran to the window to look at the Rices' barn, which was only 500 feet away, breathlessly expecting to see it burst into flames. But we could see nothing in the driving rain.

Within only a few minutes of the boom, the storm diminished as rapidly as it had begun. The wind stopped, and the bright afternoon sun suddenly burst out as if someone had turned on an electric light. Looking at the clock, we couldn't believe that the storm, which had seemed to go on for hours, had lasted only twenty minutes.

Still a bit shaken, Miss Goodrich suggested that we all go outdoors for a few minutes to look around.

"Look at the rainbow!" someone cried. We stared in awe at the brilliant double rainbow glowing in the black eastern sky amid the final sprinkles of rain and jagged flashes of distant lightning.

"Look at the barn," Charlie called. Boards were ripped from the top peak down to the basement. "The lightning really did hit it."

It was very difficult to settle down and study for the last half hour of the afternoon. Figures of speech and Chinese exports didn't seem very interesting after such a close shave. Even the exciting bloody battle of the Alamo, which the eighth grade was discussing, appeared rather dull. After all, we had been on the fringe of Eternity and had returned from it only by the slimmest of margins.

By the time school was out, we were feeling nearly back to normal. As we left the schoolroom, the bright sunshine, the calm, freshly washed air, and the sweet-smelling earth made it seem as though the violent storm had never really happened.

"Look!" yelled Conrad Lapointe. Mr. and Mrs. Rice were standing near a dead animal that was lying in front of their barn. We quickly raced over to see their chunky young Holstein bull, which they had just dragged outside with the aid of a horse. They were awaiting the arrival of the insurance adjuster to estimate the damages.

As we examined the dead bull and the shattered barn boards, we once again trembled at the awesome force of nature.

"Rose and Lily will have a lot to talk about tonight," Leopaul Lapointe said to me in a low voice. As I walked home, I wondered who in the neighborhood would get the blame for this one.

YANKEE HEALTH

All our teachers tried to constantly make us aware of the importance of good health, and they attempted to inspire us to take better care of our bodies. Miss Reynolds, who had just arrived in the neighborhood, decided to introduce us to better dental care. "We should brush our teeth twice each day and see our dentist twice a year," she announced, holding up a chart. We looked somewhat puzzled. "How many of you see your dentist twice a year?" she went on. No hands went up. "Once a year?" Still no hands. Even after a hopeful "Ever?" there were still no hands. In our neighborhood, most people visited the dentist once in their lives, for the purpose of having all their teeth pulled at the same time.

Nearly every teacher instituted early in the year some kind of inspection program that was intended to upgrade our grooming practices. Every morning, Teacher went from desk to desk, checking our hair, ears, and fingernails and looking for a comb and a clean handkerchief. Each category counted five points, if perfect. Those who scored twenty-five points each day for a week got a gold star on a chart in front of the room. Gold stars were not common, however, since most of us had uncombed hair, sometimes dirty ears, and dirty, chewed fingernails. Even if we had left home spotless, as I usually did under my mother's careful scrutiny, a few minutes of wrestling in the dirt of the schoolyard changed that. The daily health inspection became one more discouraging project for our teachers, and it was usually abandoned long before the Christmas recess.

The girls were always afraid of getting lice, and every new family that moved into the area was suspected of harboring them. Although some folks who stayed only a short time in the back country were earthy and none too hygienic, I never got lice from them or heard of anyone in our school who did. We felt lucky, because the locally accepted treatment of shaving the head and soaking it in kerosene or turpentine sounded most unpleasant.

During the winter, many girls and a few boys wore around their necks little bags filled with potions containing gum camphor or some other smelly concoction to ward off sickness. But, like the rest of us, they endured their full share of mumps, measles, chicken pox, whooping cough, and a perennial cold.

Each pupil who reached the fourth grade and beyond was required to study a health course each year. It was called "hygiene," "physiology," or whatever name was in vogue at the State Board of Education. Each book for these courses had been carefully censored by the publishers for the eyes of grammar school pupils, and although they included lavish pictures and complete descriptions of the digestive, respiratory, and circulatory systems, the reproductive area was omitted completely. We were tremendously curious about it, but that subject had to be handled in the schoolyard.

Our neighborhood always seemed to have more respect for poor health than for good, and sickness was considered a cross we should ungrudgingly bear. Even small children liked to talk about their own illnesses and those of their families. If a person was merely feeling poorly, but sending for a doctor wasn't contemplated, he was often described as being "sick abed in the woodbox" and not worthy of further discussion.

Absenteeism from school because of sickness was common, and the illnesses were usually real, since our parents were hard to fool. The teacher was also our school nurse, and if anyone took "hard sick" at school, some child was dispatched to fetch a parent to come and get him.

The second most popular topic of conversation among

the local men and women—after gossip—was their own or their family's poor health. Sickly children got a lot of sympathy, and some people stayed sickly all their lives to take advantage of the benefits. It was risky to ask anyone over age twenty how he or she was feeling, especially if you were in a hurry. Invariably you could count on spending a half hour listening to a detailed description of the person's current ill health.

"Not good" and "No better" were standard replies to the query "How are ya?" "Every mornin' I wake up is like a brand-new resurrection to me," claimed old Mrs. Jones. Even though she never had a well day in her life, she outlived several of her doctors and all her children and died at age ninety-seven. If anyone answered, "Tolerable," or "Fair-to-middlin'," it usually meant they felt they might last until noon, unless something drastic occurred.

Nearly every grown-up in my neighborhood had either a bad back, rheumatism, neuritis, a weak stomach, a rupture, a bad leg, or a lame shoulder. There were many other popular ailments, too, most of which had been diagnosed by studying the almanac or an ancient medical book. Most people mentioned proudly that they had been sickly as children: "Nobody thought I'd live."

The "frail" men worked eight or ten hours in the field or woods every day, and at least another four in the barn. The "ailing" women prepared three big meals and baked tons of bread, cakes, and pies. They made dozens of doughnuts, canned enough garden sass to fill an entire pantry each summer, churned, knit mittens, and washed by hand for a whole family. They scrubbed floors, mended, ironed, rendered lard, made over clothes, sewed quilts, and looked after the hens and pigs. They papered rooms, cared for their children and husband, put up lunches, cleaned the kerosene lamps, and on and on.

Everyone had firm beliefs about proper health habits. I was warned frequently that night air was poisonous and that to sleep in a room with an open window was to court disaster. Some folks believed that to be outdoors in the light of the full moon was to invite lunacy. The sun was also bad for you, so you should always wear a straw hat in summer. Swimming could quickly ruin your health, especially if the water was cool, as it always was in our climate. Beauty sleep could be acquired only in the hours before midnight, and any sleep after that magic hour was not nearly as beneficial.

I don't remember hearing any warnings that any kind of food was bad for me, and I took advantage of that fact to eat huge amounts of sweet desserts. However, special attributes were assigned to certain foods. "Eating meat makes you strong, sugar makes you sweet, and fish is a brain food." "Eggs make you sexy," the older kids said. Carrots would make your hair curl and help you see in the dark. Lots of salt was good for you, and if you ate burned food, you'd become pretty. Cigarettes were jokingly called coffin nails, but few took that statement seriously.

During her reign, Miss Demars, our city-born teacher, posted a large, colorful chart on the back wall of the school-room telling us what foods we must eat to keep healthy. Included were meats, eggs, milk, and bread. There were pictures of fresh fruit, including bananas, pineapples, grapefruit, and grapes, as well as fresh leafy lettuce and orange juice. We Depression children who lived miles from the nearest store snorted at the chart. Horseradish, cod liver oil, apples, canned vegetables, and berries had to supply any vitamins not included in our staple foods throughout the long winter.

The winter diet of most people consisted of large amounts of beans, potatoes, salt pork, bread, and maple syrup. The hens often didn't lay eggs in the winter, and the cows gave little milk. Since there were no refrigerators, and few people had iceboxes, in warm weather there were frequent illnesses caused by spoiled milk, moldy bread, and improperly canned vegetables. In the interest of thrift, bad meat was not always discarded, and some of our neighbors believed that if a sick cow or chicken was butchered a few minutes before it was about to die naturally, the meat would be safe to eat.

Strange ideas about clothing were often hazardous to Yankee health. When a man got dressed up for a winter church service or funeral, even if it happened to be a freezing, blizzardy day, he took off his heavy woolens and put on a lightweight summer suit. At the other extreme, many men wore dark-colored long-sleeved shirts, long underwear, and bib overalls all summer. Because a few neighborhood women still considered bare limbs sinful, they wore long dresses with long sleeves even in the warmest weather.

Nearly everyone wore shoes that were far too small, because big feet were considered shameful and were often laughed at. I used to wonder if some of the older generation had gotten their bad dispositions from painful feet. Nearly every adult had corns, calluses, bunions, and blisters, and many of those over age fifty suffered from leg ulcers. When people went out in public, they took off their too-small everyday footwear and put on even smaller dress-up shoes. A lot of the long, sad faces at funerals may have been caused more by aching feet than by grief for the deceased.

Bad backs were another common complaint, often caused by the feather beds or straw-filled mattresses everyone slept on and by the fact that men and women lifted heavy loads as a matter of course. Many bragged incessantly about all the hard work they had done when they were young and healthy.

Other common causes of ill health were the polluted wells that were dug near the backyard privy or barnyard. Some families got their water from a nearby brook whenever their springs went dry. Men worked hard all day, sweating profusely as they cut wood or gathered sap. Then they stopped to eat lunch in the cold open air or returned home in a breezy open sled.

We all had measles, whooping cough, mumps, and chicken pox before we had completed the fourth grade. The doctor or town health officer put a red-lettered quarantine sign on the door whenever anyone in the house had a contagious disease. Although it was meant to be a warning to

others, it seemed to be ignored by everyone except the peddlers. This worked so well that the Hudsons and a few others
always kept all their old signs and put them up when they
heard there was a salesman in the neighborhood.

Diphtheria, tuberculosis, and dysentery were still
around, although they were not as widespread as they had
been earlier in the century. Even a light fever always caused
alarm, because we often heard of people getting infantile
paralysis and typhoid fever, and every winter someone in the
neighborhood had influenza and pneumonia. There were people still living nearby, including the Brock sisters, who had
survived a smallpox epidemic.

In addition to sickness, people frequently had to cope
with accidents. Working with horses and cattle was especially dangerous, and each year someone got a broken leg,
cuts, or a cracked head as he misjudged his skills or misunderstood the animals. An accident, like a sickness, was often
considered a badge of honor, however, and most people enjoyed the attention a wound provided. "Had ten stitches tak-
en," folks would say admiringly of a neighbor, as if he had just
won the Iron Cross. "I cut myself right through to the bone
and almost bled to death," Hiram Forge used to say proudly.

Jed Prior cut his arm on a buzz saw one day, and when
he was being sewn up, he asked the doctor to put in at least
fifteen stitches.

"Why?" demanded the doctor.

"Well, my wife had eleven when she had her operation,
and my brother-in-law had twelve in his automobile accident,
and I want to shut 'em both up," he said.

Although dentists were not popular, doctors, surprisingly, were greatly trusted and called upon frequently, not
only for home-birthed babies but also for most serious illnesses and accidents. Dr. Buck, our family physician, was
such a kindly old soul that everyone felt better as soon as he
drove into the yard. He had to travel twelve miles each way
to reach us, and sometimes in winter we met his car on the
plowed main road down in the valley and fetched him the

two miles up our hill by sleigh. He nearly always did the treating at home and returned several times, if necessary, until his patient was well, charging three or four dollars per visit. His bill for delivering a home-born baby was more expensive; that cost $25.

Each doctor always left a big variety of pills and ointments in addition to his advice. Everyone seemed to enjoy taking medicine, and the more different-colored pills he left, the more the patient felt he was getting his money's worth. People didn't mind using salves and powders, either, but they almost never took the doctor's advice. Many times he told them to get a little rest and eat less, or to keep warm and dry, stop smoking, or eat different foods. Although his warnings went unheeded, the patient always took his placebos, usually with great results.

Many remnants of the days before a doctor was available were still around our home. Our bookcase held several old medical guides, including one for both horses and people. I read them, half believing their lore and wondering if, as one of them claimed, "For every malady Nature hands to man and beast, somewhere in field and forest she provides a cure."

Luckily, I was not afflicted with any of the disorders in the book—luckily because I would have been tempted to gather unknown roots and berries and would probably have poisoned myself in short order. I was especially glad I didn't have heartburn, because one old book offered the Indian remedy of swallowing a fishworm alive. The worm, so the book said, effectively cured heartburn and prevented it from ever returning. I wondered if my great-grandparents had ever tried that one.

Although bunches of herbs hung from the rafters in our attic, no one remembered any longer what they were or how they should be used. My grandfather had gathered them a half century before as treatment for some sickness or other. Our bookcase held nearly as many bottles as books. These, too, were filled with herbs that had been boiled and laced with whiskey, and they were on tap for any emergency. Most were home-concocted and unlabeled, but there were also some old patent medicine bottles with intriguing names like "Dr. Kilmer's Swamp Root," a magic elixir that promised to cure everything from colic to tuberculosis.

Although many aspects of healthful living may have been ignored by my family, they felt that cleanliness was next to godliness. As a child, I thought Ma was convinced that cleanliness might be even better. Every room in each house from cellar to shed chamber got its furniture moved out and a thorough scrubbing twice a year. If at any time an emergency interrupted the fall routine, a woman felt guilty if she didn't clean the house twice the next spring. Even if I was perfectly clean, I had to wash thoroughly if I went anywhere, whether to school, a neighbor's, or to the village store. We each had a bath on Saturday night, followed by clean clothes. No exceptions. My mother did not consider a summer washup in the pond or brook a substitute for a hot bath with plenty of smelly Lifebuoy soap, either.

Only one home in our neighborhood had running hot water hooked up to the woodstove, which was a very modern idea. Most families, like ours, had cold spring water that ran into the kitchen sink. A few of our neighbors had a hand pump indoors to get water from a well in the cellar, but one family had to hand-pump all their water in the front yard and carry it indoors. The handle of the pump was pulled up after each use so all the water would run back into the well and the pump would not freeze. That meant that for the next use the pump had to be primed by pouring a bit of water into the top, and if anyone forgot to put aside a few pints of water for this purpose, they had to find a bit somewhere or else melt some snow before the pump could be used.

We were lucky enough to have a spring on the hill behind the house. Water ran into the house by gravity, so I never learned the pump-priming routine. We still had to heat water on the wood stove, however, and we used a large copper washboiler when a great deal was needed for laundry or baths. Like most people we bathed beside the kitchen stove in a large galvanized tub, pulling the shades and covering the window in the door as best we could. My brothers and sisters got first chances at bathing, so it was some time before it was my turn. Although in some households the same water was used for several baths before being changed, Ma made sure we always got fresh hot water for each scrub.

In spite of my mother's insistence on cleanliness and diet, I was never convinced that we were any healthier than the nine Temple children who lived in a two room paper shack and probably had never taken a real bath in their life. When I brought this up to Ma, however, I was quickly informed that any discussion about the merits of fewer baths was useless, and no matter how few the pennies, there would be no economizing on soap.

SPRING HOOKY

None of us ever thought seriously of "playing hooky," as the funny papers called skipping school. We knew that the consequences would be too awful: capture by the truant officer or a county sheriff and then, as one boy described it, "an eight-year scholarship to the Reform School." Only if we could prove we were hard sick were we allowed to stay home, but never merely to work or because of bad weather, and certainly never to go fishing. That is why what happened on a May day in the middle-1930s made no sense. There was no precedent for it, and it never happened again as long as I was part of School District 9.

The morning started with a bright sunrise in the clear sky, and everywhere there was the unmistakable fragrance and feel of spring. Our chickens, cattle, and even the cats and the dog seemed to enjoy the sensation of life returning after the long months of snow. Daffodils were finally sprouting, the robins and crows had returned from the south, and tiny reddish-yellow leaves had begun to form on the maple trees.

It felt good to carry my jacket over my arm on the way to school instead of wearing it, and I happily ran most of the way. The salute to the flag was still being held inside, according to our winter custom, so we were cheated out of an extra few seconds in the morning sun. I spent a lot of time staring out the windows that morning, and it was especially difficult to concentrate on the Battle of Manila Bay and learn the capitals of the South American countries.

At morning recess we played Prisoner's Base more vigorously than we had anytime since the snow melted. When the teacher shook her bell, we dragged in reluctantly and struggled painfully through interminable lessons of spelling, reading, and long division. The recitations droned on as the hands on the old Regulator clock turned ever so slowly toward noon. It was one of the longest mornings of my school years, and never had the outdoors beckoned more invitingly. Once when a couple of crows fluttered by the window, Roger Lincoln whispered to me, "I think they're going on a picnic." I wondered whimsically if he had noticed some lunch baskets, and I dreamily speculated about what it would be like to be a high-flying bird on a perfect May morning.

When the teacher finally announced lunchtime, the dozen of us, released from prison at last, moved more rapidly than ever before. For the first time that spring, we all rushed outside to gulp down our sandwiches in the bright sunshine.

It seemed foolish to play silly games, so we ran around exuberantly, chasing one another, tossing off the chains of winter as we had earlier thrown off our heavy coats and boots. With each wide circle we made, we ran farther from the schoolhouse and, with no idea how it happened, were soon in George Tyler's maple woods. The bright sun shone brilliantly through the nearly naked limbs of the maples as we ran over the forest floor, just beginning to come alive with violets, mayflowers, and wild onions. Above the rustling noise we made in the damp leaves of last autumn, we could hear birds singing, chipmunks calling, and the occasional distant drumming of a romantic partridge.

Intoxicated with spring, we floated dreamily, without direction, like moths out of our cocoons, first one way and then another. Boys and girls ran together, led by a mysterious, unseen Pied Piper. We saw squirrels running along old stone walls, and a woodchuck standing beside his hole stared curiously at us. But no one said, "I wish I had a gun." The animals were part of the enchanted forest that day, and probably if a bear had stood up and waved a greeting, none of us would have been surprised.

Leaving the maple woods, we ran into the dark green balsam forest, where it was deliciously cool, moist, and fragrant. We found an old cellar hole among the tall evergreens, and nearby, two homemade tombstones with hand lettering crudely carved on them. "Age two years," was all we could read. Jack Hudson had seen them before, because the woods belonged to his uncle. He told us that they were twins, distant relatives of his, who had died in a diphtheria epidemic during the Civil War.

As we traced the foundations of the house, the barn, and some of the outbuildings by searching carefully among the trees, I wondered about the people who had lived here. They probably spent a lifetime or two clearing that land before they moved and gave it back to the wilderness. Would the forest one day quietly erase the farm where my family had lived for more than a century? Would our schoolhouse also disappear into the great North Woods? A hundred years from now, would it look as if no one had ever been there?

The thoughts were fleeting, rather than depressing, as they might have been at another time. We were too busy splashing through spring puddles to worry; and to our surprise, in one cool, shady spot we found a small pile of dark-colored snow and had one last, but very half-hearted, snowball fight.

Finally, with our energy greatly diminished, we suddenly realized we were a long way from the schoolhouse. Since only Jack knew the way back, he slowly led the little band of truants out of the forest. A flock of geese in a big *V* formation passed over us, flying north lazily, as we crossed the open field in back of the school. Like the geese, we felt no need to hurry.

Oddly, none of us felt any sense of guilt as we entered the schoolhouse, eager to tell all about our adventures. We were stunned when we saw that the hands on the old Regulator clock pointed to nearly two o'clock, indicating that we were more than an hour late. Ordinarily the teacher would have been extremely upset and would have punished us with double-time to be made up and notes to our parents recommending more punishment at home. But instead she gave us only a brief talk telling us it was not a nice thing to do. Then she resumed our lessons. Perhaps we looked too exhilarated and innocent to be chastised. More likely, Miss Reynolds, who was barely twenty-one herself, got the same message that spring morning that we did, and as she saw us disappear into the woods, felt a little sad that her training and position kept her from running with us.

THE BLUE AND THE GRAY

Memorial Day, or "Decoration Day," as most of the older citizens still called it, was an occasion for another school performance. Although only five or six mothers, neighbors, and a few small children attended, the day would have been observed whether anyone came or not.

Unlike the Christmas or Halloween programs, which we pupils enjoyed very much, none of us liked Memorial Day's event at all. Our aversion to the program was not because we were unpatriotic or disrespectful, but because we hated the awful drills, pieces, and songs that we were made to repeat year after year. At that time, our country had been involved in at least four French and Indian wars, the Revolutionary War, the War of 1812, the Mexican War, the Spanish-American War, World War I, and numerous skirmishes with Barbary pirates and western Indians. One would never have guessed, however, by listening to our annual program that these historical events had occurred. The ancient and tattered book we used each year apparently had been written by someone who was acquainted only with the Civil War.

Everything in the book had to do with the Blue and the Gray. The songs included "Tenting Tonight," "Battle Cry of Freedom," "Tramp, Tramp, Tramp," and "Just Before the Battle, Mother." We would have preferred some peppy marching songs like "Over There" or even "Yankee Doodle," but they weren't in the book, so that was that. By the time any of us reached the fifth grade, we knew all the songs and pieces by heart, and I'm sure everyone in the neighborhood who attended our program each year knew them too.

Although our teachers tried to put some polish into the event and insisted that we dress in our best clothes, it had little drama. We always said the pieces in monotonous sing-song voices, befitting the somber subject that we found difficult to comprehend. One girl was assigned to learn the classic "The Blue and the Gray" by Francis Miles French. In spite of the teacher's best efforts, she recited it with no feeling, and in a lilting voice that fell at the end of each line:

> Under the sod and the dew,
> Waiting the Judgment Day,
> Under the one the Blue,
> Under the tother the Gray.

We always learned the pieces thoroughly, because to forget them on the big day would be disgraceful to us, the teacher, and our mothers. Teacher copied the parts carefully from the tattered old book so we could take them home, and we recited them to our families, the cows, and the chickens, all of whom showed little more interest than we.

Sometimes a teacher attempted a small break with tradition. Mrs. Marshall, in her first year with us, had us create a beautiful grave from evergreen boughs and place it with a white wooden cross at the front of the schoolroom. Unfortunately, because it had never been part of our traditional ceremony, it confused us, and several children moving into place for their pieces and drills fell over it. By the next year she was better indoctrinated and faithfully stuck with the book and the ancient rituals.

Another year an adventuresome teacher decided that the World War was worthy of a mention in our program, so she found a copy of a poem she liked, "In Flanders Field" by John McCrae. Although it was beautiful as the teacher read it, Rosanna Mudd, who was chosen to recite it, was rather young.

She learned the words well but recited them without expression, and they came out in a dull, lifeless monotone. When she started the second verse, her barely audible voice sounded weak and ready to fade away.

"We are the dead," she began sleepily.

"Most convincing speech I ever heard in this school," I heard one mother whisper to another.

Each of us was assigned at least one recitation to say alone. They varied from a simple poem about the glorious red, white, and blue to the Gettysburg Address, which was delivered by the most capable speaker each year. Although I got a crack at most of the pieces, I never had the honor of tackling that one. Nor was I chosen to dramatize Whittier's "Barbara Frietchie" and her bout with Stonewall Jackson:

> Shoot if you must this old gray head
> But spare your country's flag, she said.

I might as well have recited them, since hearing the endless repetitions bore the lines into my brain forever.

The individual pieces were interspersed with songs and exercises or "drills," as they were usually called. Since we all took part in at least two or three, the program was not short. In a proper "drill," three or four boys or girls paraded in front of the audience with signs, flags, or flowers, Each child said a short poem separately, and the group then chanted a few lines in chorus, sometimes waving a flag. Although the drills had long been a traditional part of every country school's Memorial Day program, they were no doubt as painful to watch as they were to perform. We went through the oft-repeated phrases in a dreary manner, looking out the window frequently and envying the squirrels and chipmunks, which didn't have to stay inside and speak pieces. The monotony of the day was broken only by unscheduled events such as the time Foster Waugh, who was very large for his age and somewhat awkward, accidentally knocked over little Annie Markres, who always stood on her tiptoes during the songs so she would be as tall as Rose Barker. She promptly slugged him.

Another year Babe Gillson got whooping cough in the middle of May and missed the entire two weeks before Memorial Day, so he had to learn his speech at home without benefit of the teacher's tutelage. Unfortunately, no one explained otherwise, so he carefully memorized the stage directions along with his speech. On the big day the distressed teacher stared helplessly as he repeated the instructions at different points throughout the poem. He said, "Holds up flag," "Waves flag," "Jumps up and down happily," rather than actually doing any of them.

A few days later, on the real Decoration Day, I went on the annual pilgrimage with my family to the cemetery near the village. We took bouquets of daffodils, lilacs, and apple blossoms in old glass jars and placed them on the graves of our ancestors—including my grandfather, who had been at Gettysburg. All around us in the cemetery we could see fresh new flags on little stakes that designated stones of the veterans of various wars. I left my family and ran from one to the other to read the epitaphs. "Died at Andersonville." "Killed in action at The Battle of the Wilderness." "Died of smallpox in Virginia." Suddenly our history lessons became more vivid, and the Memorial Day songs and poetry had some meaning. I resolved, the year I was in sixth grade, that the next May I would try to talk the teacher into producing a more worthwhile program.

My enthusiasm didn't last for twelve months, however, and tradition reigned, as it had for decades. The next Memorial Day exercises were unchanged, and 1935's program was very likely much like the one in 1902.

PICNIC

By the first of June, we were all thoroughly sick of the inside of the schoolhouse. The days were very warm, and our dull, bleak room just couldn't compete with the outdoors. We talked about little except summer vacation and the upcoming school picnic. Our families rarely took time to go on picnics, so this event was always a special treat. For countless years, the last day of school in mid-June had been the traditional date, and it always took place in George Tyler's maple woods.

We went to school as usual that day, and after morning exercises the teacher collected our books, pencils, and erasers and handed us our end-of-year report cards. We took them apprehensively, dreading the news that we might be back in the same grade for another year. Although we never showed our cards to one another, the look on every child's face plainly showed what was written on the line "Promoted to Grade _____."

The subjects were graded by letters. "E" meant excellent, a letter that was awarded sparingly. "S" stood for superior, "M" for medium, "I" for inferior, and "U" for unsatisfactory, or failure. Our mothers always arrived at school by mid-morning and insisted on seeing the cards at once. Each one seemed especially interested in the category on the back of the card marked "Deportment." They carefully searched, too, for any "X" checked beside such listings as "Indolent," "Wastes Time," "Work Is Carelessly Done," "Gets Too Much Help," "Gives Up Too Easily," "Inattentive," and other such painfully revealing items. Even though they had signed the cards every six weeks throughout the school year, the mothers knew as well as we that the final term had been the last opportunity to make good. A few felt compelled to severely lecture their offspring in front of us all.

By late morning most of the other neighborhood women and their younger children had arrived with baskets of sandwiches, cookies, cakes, and jugs of lemonade made with real lemons. Their arrival signaled that it was time to start our short hike into the woods. The morning dew had long since evaporated from the fern-covered earth; and the maple trees, decked out with fresh new leaves, gave a lush, green look to everything. Spring had already given way to summer, so the shade of the maples felt good.

By the time I was in the seventh grade I felt quite grown up, and the school picnic was a lot less exciting. Miss Reynolds and the other women spread out the food as we ran about, tipping over small dead trees and playing I-Spy and tag among the evergreens on the fringe of the hardwood forest. This was interrupted when the teacher, feeling that we needed some structured play, called us together to organize a scavenger hunt for wildflowers and bird feathers and offered bits of colored ribbon for prizes. We played her game with only half-hearted enthusiasm, because we could see the delicious goodies spread out on the white tablecloth on the ground and had no intention of searching too far afield for anything as silly as bird feathers. Finally, after what seemed an eternity to a hungry schoolboy, lunch was ready, and we ate sitting on rocks, fallen logs, and stumps.

It felt good not to be one of the little kids any more, but also a little strange, with no bigger boys around to look to as models. It was frightening, too, just thinking about growing up in a most unfamiliar world.

Our area was changing rapidly. Only three of the original fourteen one-room schools in our township were now in operation, and there was talk that these would close within a few years, and the pupils would be sent to the village school. Everywhere, bigger was becoming better. Little stores and shops that had been around for more than a century were closing. Some were refusing to stock the unfamiliar Ovaltine, Tastyeast, and other new products being advertised on the radio, so people went elsewhere. Also, many farmers now had better cars and were finding it more exciting to go to a larger town to do their shopping. Many small farms were going out of business, finding it difficult to comply with the new milk regulations.

As my schoolmates and I grew up, the whole world seemed to be changing, too. Events that occurred thousands of miles away now seemed to be reshaping our lives and futures. We were hearing unfamiliar, disquieting words such as "income tax," "consolidation," "Social Security," "refugees," "Maginot Line," "standardization," "dive bomber," "submarine," "aircraft carrier," "bomb shelter," "blitz," and "ersatz." Everyone talked a lot about Hitler and war. The Rhineland had been occupied, the Nazi Air Force was fast becoming the world's best, threats were being made to Austria, and our superhero, Charles Lindbergh, was making puzzling statements about the Third Reich.

But we had other heroes, like Amelia Earhart, Wiley Post, Lou Gehrig, Will Rogers, Richard Byrd, Babe Ruth, Joe Louis, and even, for a while, Huey Long. My pulse quickened when I read of balloon trips into the stratosphere, autogyros, and 'round-the-world flights, and I could hardly wait to fly a plane.

We talked endlessly about roadsters, Mickey Mouse, Mae West, Guy Lombardo, Amos 'n' Andy, Charlie McCarthy, and the crazy new clothes and dances. Carefully and sheepishly, I kept a picture of Ginger Rogers hidden in my history book for months. I wanted desperately to write to her, but I didn't know how.

Although most of us had still scarcely been beyond the bounds of our own small county, we read eagerly in our new current event papers of giant ocean liners, tall buildings that reached into the clouds, drive-in theatres, and musical movies. At home our Atwater-Kent radio with its three large batteries let us in on the happenings of the world, sometimes nearly as soon as they occurred. Each week we hung on "The March of Time" as it dramatically portrayed the week's happenings in an exciting "You are there" manner. Lowell Thomas kept us informed each evening in his powerful, organlike voice, and we were all ears as King Edward gave up the great British Empire for the woman he loved. Late at night I listened dreamily to Big Bands and popular songs from such faraway places as Boston and New York.

But on the school picnic in Mr. Tyler's maple woods, my thoughts were concerned mostly with my final year in elementary school and the fast-approaching summer. For two-and-a-half months, we boys knew that we would have to work for weeks in the hayfields, our hot, sweaty bodies covered with itchy hay chaff, black flies, and dust. I knew it would be bearable only because of the few welcome breaks.

First, there would be a family reunion on the Fourth of July with lots of food and firecrackers. Then there would be our annual trip to the county fair in Barton, with its high-flying flags, big tents, Ferris wheel, and other exciting rides. The barns would be filled with sheep, cattle, and horses, and I'd smell the unfamiliar aromas of cigar smoke, baled straw, and cooking hamburgers. We would stare open-mouthed at the trapeze artists, gymnasts, and jugglers and marvel at the skill of the school bands and sulky drivers.

On warm, misty July evenings at home, the valley below our house would be filled with thousands of fireflies putting on their own spectacular display of fireworks. I had hoped that this summer I would have time for more swims and a fishing trip, and I knew we would have homemade root beer, ice cream, and wild-strawberry shortcakes. Although I felt happy that the seventh grade was over, I knew I would miss my schoolmates, especially on lonely Saturday nights and Sunday afternoons, when I was certain a whole world was out having fun, except for me.

My last school picnic, when I was in the eighth grade, was the most memorable. I was nearly thirteen and felt very adult, having spent two years in a back seat. Our little school had so few students that it was now scheduled to close for certain the following year. Since half of us now had back seats, the anticipated prestige was missing.

For the first time in decades, the annual picnic was not to be held in Tyler's maple woods, and our mothers and neighbors wouldn't be there. Jean Lapointe had offered to take us all to the beach at Caspian Lake in his new farm truck.

After the teacher had handed us our report cards, we piled into the truck, standing up so we could see above the high sideboards and so the wind would blow hard into our faces. At the beach we dug wells in the sand and stared at the lake, which was a deep blue and covered with rippling waves that made it look as if the whole shoreline were moving. We waded in the cold water, skipped flat pebbles over it, and watched the little minnows that came close to shore. Now and then we saw a canoe or rowboat glide by.

As we sat on the cement dock to eat our paper-bag lunches, several boys and girls from the nearby high school came to eat theirs on the granite boulders a short distance from us. After they had finished, a tall, slim girl walked over to talk with us. She was sixteen, she said, and, I thought, stunningly beautiful. She talked with us a while, then rejoined her group as they headed back to school. As she left, I completely forgot about Ginger Rogers. For the first time in my life, I was head over teakettle in love and no longer dreading the unfamiliar village high school. Badly smitten, I stared after her until she was out of sight. My eyes suddenly filled with flashing stars, and I turned and walked off the cement dock into the cold lake and into the future.

USEFUL YANKEE EXPRESSIONS

Ayuh or **ayer** Affirmative answer, meaning "yes," that is used occasionally. "Wal, maybe" is a more cautious and much more common response.

Croncher Large, such as, "That log is an old croncher."

Doaw A strong negative word, used in answering a question such as "Are you going to support the drive to build a new school?"

Fit Past tense of fight.

Grange Rural organization noted for its community service, dinners, and card parties.

Hay mow A pile of loose hay stored in the barn to feed cattle and horses; sometimes used for socializing by young couples.

Het Heated water, food, or people can get het up.

Honker Large; can be used in place of croncher.

I gory A common expression.

I snum Another expression; like "I gory," it adds flavor to conversation and allows the speaker time to think of the phrase that will follow it. "By crimus" is another useful by-word.

Little snot Anyone under six years old.

Meetin' Common word for church. "He hain't been ta meetin' since nobody can remember."

Obliged Used instead of thanks. "I'm much obliged for the cider."

Old pelter Anyone older than you are.

On him A term explaining an unexpected event, and usually one that didn't actually occur *on* the person described. "Hiram's cow up and got sick on him."

Smarten up To straighten out verbally a person who has got his facts considerably mixed up.

Stave To make a big commotion so it will look like you are working.

Stand for Run for a public office.

Sugar Place A grove of maple trees where maple syrup is produced. It also contains the *sugar house,* where the maple sap is cooked into the syrup.

Supper Evening meal. Dinner is et at noon, prompt. Lunch is carried to work in a bucket.

To Popular prefix, such as, "He's to bed" or "She ain't to home," often slurred to sound like *tabed* or *ta home.*

Took and Sentence extender. "I took and brung in a load of shavings yesterday." "Pa took and got sick."

Up and Substitute for *took and.* "Henry's hoss up and died on him."

Vaw Expression of disapproval. Pointing a finger at the same time adds emphasis.

Vittles or victuals Prepared food that's ready to be et.

Wed Past tense of weed. "I wed the garden before I et supper."